APRIL SCOTT

BEHIND
THE
BRIEFCASE

ZaaGaa Productions
ZGP

Behind The Briefcase

Copyright 2008 by April Scott
Published by ZaaGaa Productions, Inc.
www.zaagaaproductions.com
Distributed by Midpoint Trade Books, Inc.

Library of Congress Cataloging-in-Publication Data
Scott, April.
Behind the Briefcase/ April Scott. —1st pbk. ed.
Beverly Hills, Calif.: ZaaGaa Productions, 2008

ISBN 13: 978-0-9815350-0-5
ISBN 10: 0-9815350-0-3
Printed and bound in the United States of America
Cover photo by Josh Silberman
Cover photo editing by Ken Matthews

While the author and publisher have made every effort to ensure the
accuracy and completeness of information contained in this book, we
assume no responsibility for errors, inaccuracies, omissions, or any
inconsistency herein. Any slights of people, places, or organizations are
unintentional. Further publisher does not have any control over and does not
assume any responsibility for author or third-party Websites or their content.

ATTENTION CORPORATIONS, UNIVERSITIES, COLLEGES, AND
PROFESSIONAL ORGANIZATIONS: Quantity discounts are available on
bulk purchases of this book for educational, gift purposes, or as premiums
for increasing magazine subscriptions or renewals. Special books or book
excerpts can also be created to fit specific needs. For information, please
contact ZaaGaa Productions, P.O. Box 5775, Beverly Hills, CA 90209; ph
310-858-8410.

To my family and friends. Thank you for all your love and support. And to Julian-- Always.

Contents

PART 3: HOW TO GET ON DEAL OR NO DEAL

AFTERWARD

APPENDIX: FREQUENTLY ASKED QUESTIONS

ABOUT THE AUTHOR

THE REAL DEAL

Who am I?

My name is April Scott. I was model #14 on the hit NBC gameshow *Deal or No Deal* for 38 episodes. I'm basically a small town girl who moved to Hollywood five years ago to try and make it big.

What's in this Book?

I begin with a brief history of myself, primarily for those of you who might be interested in a career in the entertainment industry. Perhaps my experiences moving from Missouri to California will be of some use to you. Or at the very least, offer some encouragement. I remember how it felt to be unfulfilled; believing deep down that I could accomplish more with my life, but realizing that my dreams were unbelievably far out of reach.

So, for those of you who might know what that feels like, and for those of you who might still be searching; I offer my story.

I will also lead you through my entire *Deal or No Deal* experience. You will walk with me through the audition process, the wardrobe fittings, and even accompany me in the private Hair, Makeup, and Dressing rooms. You will get a glimpse of what really goes on (on *and* off the stage), get to know the other Briefcase Babes, and learn inside information about the show itself.

I have also included a detailed section on how to be hired as a briefcase model and tips on becoming a *Deal or No Deal* contestant.

I've made every attempt to be factual, unbiased, and brutally honest.

And this is how it really was....Behind The Briefcase.

PART 1

FROM A GRAVEL ROAD
TO RODEO DRIVE

CHAPTER 1

DOWN ON THE FARM

I grew up in the outskirts of Campbell, Missouri. It was a rural town of roughly 2000 people tucked away and forgotten in the southeastern corner of the state that was referred to as the "bootheel." The area was mostly flat land with lots of farms and friendly people. The winters were cold, wet, and dreary. The summers were hot and humid, and the mosquitoes swarm so thick after dusk that they would nearly pick you up and carry you away. The springs and falls were lovely.

We lived three miles down an old gravel road on a twenty acre farm with cows, a large barn, and a pond. There were lots of tall trees, singing birds, fresh air, and pretty flowers (that my parents would grow), but it was an isolated and lonely place to grow up. I had no neighboring children to play with, only farm cats and my imagination. But I amused myself. I would fish, wander through the thickets and the fields, and search through our barn for interesting finds. The barn was like a gypsy's back pocket. My dad, the constant collector of all things unusual or old, had filled it with: old bicycles, oil lanterns, rusted toy train sets, boxes of old magazines from the 1950's and 1960's, thousands of books, old chairs, tables, beds (all awaiting refinishing or repair), and bits and pieces of anything and everything else. It was always fun to explore.

Our house was a museum, filled to the brim with antiques and collectibles. A wooden phone booth sat in the basement (and it actually worked). Beside it was an upright player piano. (I was told that it *used* to work, but it hadn't since I was born.) Glassware, old books, Victrolas (antique record players), a collection of Indian arrowheads (that were found in our fields), paintings, pictures, quilts, vintage hats, and old phones covered our shelves, our tables, and every inch of our walls. Every item had a story, which might have entertained an adult, but not so much a child.

We had three TV channels. Cable TV wasn't available out in the country where we lived, and only CBS was clear. If you wanted to watch the other two networks, you needed to walk outside around the north side of the house and twist the antenna pole to the opposite direction. My father worked as a Telephone Repairman (which explains his collection of phones), and my mom was a Secretary for our local bank. They were both creative and very intelligent. They too were born and raised in Campbell, and like most other natives; they had remained there. No one seemed to stray far from that little town. It was a magnet with an invisible pull, both subtle and slow, but constant. We bought our groceries from the grocery store, and everything else from Wal-Mart. No one that I knew personally had ever been to California. Why I was ready to move here, from as far back as

I can remember; I can't quite say. But I've always wanted to be an actress.

I grew up watching, *The Wizard of Oz,* and, *Gone with the Wind*, and identifying very closely with Dorothy and Scarlet (as I suppose most girls do). But the excitement I felt when I watched them on the screen felt so personal. It was as if I had either experienced it before, or that somehow I knew I would experience it in the future. I decided that being in movies was the best job in the whole world. Movies were magical, and living in such an isolated environment on the farm, made me want magic in my life.

My childhood was fairly uneventful. I attended the local public school, and I remember spending most of my free time reading (mainly Nancy Drew books), practicing piano, and playing Little League softball in the summers. Even though I led an ordinary life, throughout my childhood, I always believed (mostly in secret) that I was someone special, and that I was destined for great things. Even if, no one else knew it at the time.

My early teenage years were filled with rebellion. I wore mostly black clothes and ripped Levis. My favorite bands were, "Guns and Roses," "Metallica," and "The Doors." My boyfriend was a few years older than me and was always in and out of trouble, (of course my parents didn't approve of that relationship). I looked for excitement in all the wrong places and even found myself expelled from school for a period of time in eighth grade for having alcohol on campus. (Yeah, that was a bad idea.) And as in most small towns, gossip spreads like wildfire; and almost at once, I was an outcast.

I was kicked off of the Freshman cheerleading team, which was basically the only activity that there was for a young teenage girl to do in my school. Being left out, made my friends in the popular crowd turn on me, and I felt even more alone. I would come home from school, lock myself in my room, listen to music and just exist. I felt alienated not only from my peers, but from my parents, my town, and my life. I was miserable. It's ironic, but a dress and my smile would be my ultimate salvation.

CHAPTER 2

MISS SOYBEAN

I got involved in beauty pageants by chance. In the summer of 1993, I happened to be flipping through our local newspaper and ran across an article about my town's beauty pageant — Jr. Miss Peach Queen. It was taking place that Friday night during our town's annual outdoor carnival called, "The Peach Fair." I had entered a few pageants when I was growing up (when I was four, five, eleven, and twelve), but I hadn't won any of them. I did get first alternate once (when I was four). The preteen pageants, that I had been in, were always uncomfortable experiences for me. I recall the pseudo pageant gowns that my mom created for me. Her head bent at the kitchen table sewing by hand well into the night: gathering pieces from my older sister's 80's prom dresses, or chopping the trains from thrift store wedding gowns. Each surgery a miraculous attempt to make a poor pitiful dress *pass* as a pageant gown; a desperation that perhaps only country people can relate to. Yes, I was hesitant to get involved in any pageant.

All that smiling didn't fit in with my rebel phase anyhow. But like most females from small towns, I couldn't shake my desire to wear a crown.

I casually mentioned it to my mom; who paused for a moment between potato peels at the kitchen sink. Probably shocked at the fact that I was taking an interest in something normal and pleasantly surprised; but her practical sensibility prevented her from endorsing a pageant as a worthwhile venture. I remember hearing phrases like: "Lots of money!" "Lots of nonsense!" and lots of, "You can be in it if you want to, but don't get your hopes up!" She set the potatoes to boil and asked me the details. I read from the paper: "For girls ages 13 to 15. Entry fee of 35 dollars. The winner will receive a rhinestone crown, a sash, a trophy, and get to ride on top of a convertible in the town's parade." I swallowed hard and looked up at her with wide eyes. Yes, we were both thinking the same secretive thought, "Wow! Who could ask for anything more than that?" Yes, pageants were big deals in small towns. They ranked right up there with pickup trucks, harvesting crops, hunting season, going to church, decorating the outside of your house with Christmas lights, and basketball games. Pageant queens were small town royalty. Outwardly, we remained detached and calm as we made a plan to drive to Poplar Bluff (the big town nearby) on the following morning to search for a dress. But inwardly, we were filled with childish enthusiasm.

We left the house around 10 o'clock with high hopes and two Dr. Peppers tucked into Koozie cups. We pulled the silver Ford Taurus station wagon (affectionately nicknamed, "The Silver Bullet," out of our driveway and onto the gravel road. As my mom tore over the hills and potholes, we decided that we would start our search at a secondhand store. We didn't know what we would find, but we weren't expecting to pay over thirty dollars.

We made a left onto the highway and headed north. We passed a large vegetable and fruit stand and a field, and then another field, and a farmhouse. Then we drove by another field, and another field, and then a great big field, and then a farmhouse. And then three more fields, a gas station, a church, a school, and another church, another gas station, and then another field. And this cycle would basically repeat when we came to the next town. That was one good thing about the bootheel: it could grow crops. Spit a watermelon seed on the ground, and next year you'll get a whole mess of watermelons in your backyard! Yes, much like the women, the soil in Dunklin country was very fertile.

Forty-five minutes later, we parked the car. The little gold bell above the door jingled over our heads as we walked inside the small quiet thrift store. The elderly woman at the counter greeted us with a smile as we scanned the room for dresses. We found a whole rack, but since I wasn't into looking like a 1976 Homecoming Queen, I was out of luck. We hit a few more thrift stores on the way out of town, but to no avail. My mom reminded me, once again, of my sister's metallic gold lemay prom dress (from 1987) still hanging in the guest room closet, but I shook my head. I was fourteen years old now, and I couldn't show up looking like an idiot this time. I was sad, but we couldn't find a dress. And that was that. And *no* dress; meant *no* pageant.

As we drove home in silence, I stared out the window at the fields, the gas station, the church, and then the pageant shop... Wait a minute—Pageant Shop? I yelled at my mom, "Stop! I just saw a sign that said "Petals and *Pageants*!" To which she replied, "Yeah, I knew that was there, but it's probably really expensive, and we can't afford to pay a lot of money just for one night." I watched her in disbelief as she barreled the station wagon down the highway. After a few seconds of gritting my teeth, I broke down and *begged* her to turn the car around. She hesitated, but finally her blinker came on as I heard her say, "Well, I guess we can just *look*."

We pulled into the gravel driveway of the shop. It was made of the fancy, sparkly, white gravel rocks, (the kind that the rich city people had in their driveways.) I was a little intimidated as my Keds tennis shoes crunched their way across to the double glass doors. The door dinged as I walked inside, but a high-class doorbell ring. It sounded electronic. And the store... It was *filled* with beautiful pageant dresses! There were little girls' dresses all the way to adult sizes, and they were all, quite simply, beautiful. I never imagined such a place. I walked over to the Jr. sizes and began browsing.

There were so many to choose from. Mom explained to the two women what I was looking for, and they began handing me gowns to try on. I was in heaven in that dressing room. I would try on a dress, step out in front of the large full-length mirror, and listen as everyone stated their opinion. After a few dozen dresses or so, we unanimously found "the one." It was a red sequined gown, and it was perfect. It had a sweetheart neckline, long sleeves, and a cutout back. But it also had a rental price of 185 dollars a night! And that was a crazy amount of money for that area, and for that sort of thing. That was a week's worth of work for most people, and I didn't have a penny to my name. But... *Dad* did. Yes, Dad! We would drive home, tell my Dad about my dilemma, convince him that we had to have this dress, and then come back and pay for it. Yes, that's just what we would do. And that's just what we did.

Mom and I lobbied my case before my Dad. And even though I'm certain that he thought we were nuts, he gave his approval. The next afternoon, we raced back, paid the money, and took the dress...plus some shoes, and some earrings...

It was Friday night and the pageant drew in a large crowd. You could feel the energy in the air as the girls waited backstage in the makeshift changing area. (They had walled in the park's concrete bandstand with ply-board and hooked up a window air-conditioning unit to stop the sweat and keep out the mosquitoes.) I remember how my heart was racing as the announcer called my number, and a woman yanked aside a curtain of metallic blue floor-length plastic strips (probably pulled from the high school's leftover prom decorations.) I walked passed her and out into the spotlights of the bandstand. I paused gracefully upon the Duct taped X on the concrete floor.

It took a moment for my eyes to adjust to the floodlights, and a second for me to block out the sounds of the screaming kids on the Swings, the jerky movements of the Zipper's cages, and the spinning Tilt-A-Whirls. But as I walked down the ramp, smiling at the trio of judges sitting across from me in lawn chairs, I might as well had been walking out to accept an Academy Award. I felt dignity for the first time in a long time. I felt special. I felt important. And even though I didn't win that night (I got in the top eight). I still had a wonderful time, because I had found something that excited me.

I told my parents just how much I had enjoyed the pageant, and that I wanted to compete in more. I had read in the newspaper of another pageant that was taking place the following weekend twenty miles away in a small town in Arkansas. Mom explained to my Dad how it would eventually be cheaper to buy the dress than to rent it again a few times. He gave her the go ahead, and they paid another six hundred dollars to buy that dress for me! It was an awful lot of money, but it was undoubtedly the best thing that they could have done for me at the time. I competed in the Arkansas pageant the next weekend—and I won!

Over the next four years, I competed in over eighty local pageants and took home 45 crowns and lots of trophies. We'd sometimes drive an hour and a half away to do a bigger pageant, but most were in the surrounding towns. Here are but a few of my distinguished titles: Miss Soybean, Miss Sweet Pea, Miss Cotton Bowl, Miss Sunflower, Miss Liberty, Miss 4th of July, and Miss St. Patrick's Day. I even managed to enter my town's pageant once again, two years later, and take home the coveted, "Miss Peach Queen," title at the age of 16. Yes, life was good. All of my pageant success really boosted my self-confidence, and by my senior year in high school, I had decided that I was ready to take the first step towards making my secret dream of becoming an actress a reality.

I made the decision to major in Theater at the University of Missouri (where my older sister was getting her Master's degree in Biological Engineering). Everything was fine, until I realized that the scholarship I had been awarded from my Dad's work (he worked as a Telephone Service Repairman for Southwestern Bell) didn't cover the Liberal Arts. And I couldn't afford to attend college without it. The scholarship covered basically every other discipline except Art, Music, and Theater. I didn't want to have to ask my parents for money for school. So, I reluctantly changed my major from Theater to Chemistry (an area I also enjoyed).

The scholarship covered my tuition expenses, but I didn't have enough leftover to pay for room and board. So, I moved in with my sister and her husband and commuted to school every day.

I realized fairly quickly that studying Chemistry was not *nearly* as exciting as I had hoped it would be. I was doing well in my classes (Physics, Biology, Rural Sociology. Yes, I did enjoy the sciences, and I was making all A's), but I was bored. I wanted to do acting. But even though *I* wasn't acting, I could, at the very least, watch *others* acting. My sister and I would attend almost every Theater Department performance. We saw everything: the musicals, the dramas, the comedies, and even the strange experimental performances. They were so exciting to watch. We loved them!

Halfway through the semester, I decided to send in an application to transfer to a small private college in southwest Missouri that was set up for low income students. It had a work study program where you could work fifteen hours a week on campus to pay your tuition. (Which honestly didn't sound too appealing to me at the time, but I was willing to do what I needed to do.) I decided that scrubbing floors would be a pretty small sacrifice if it would allow me to study acting.

One afternoon after finishing a day of classes, I got home and found a letter from the college in the mail. I took a deep breath as I opened it. They had accepted me! It was a godsend. Now, I could major in theater and still be able to afford room and board! I kissed the letter and began packing my bags.

CHAPTER 3

COLLEGE IN THE OZARKS

The College of the Ozarks was located on a secluded campus with dairy cows roaming the fields in front, and it was extremely conservative. We had to attend church on Sunday, and we had to abide by strict rules. In addition to having twenty plus course hours a semester, I was responsible for working fifteen hours a week at my on-campus job. My first job was in "maintenance." (Which is a fancy word for janitor.) After that, I was an R.A. (Resident Assistant) in a girls' dorm for two years. Then, I worked in the *Center for Writing and Thinking*; a computer lab where students wrote papers and researched on the Internet. Since we weren't allowed to have the Internet in our dorm rooms (I suppose the school was trying to protect us from its evil influences); it was a pretty cool job, and as you might imagine, a popular place.

No, the college couldn't have been further from the glitz and glamour of Hollywood, but it allowed me to major in Theater. So, I sucked it up and buckled down. I even started to enjoy it. I liked being isolated from the world. It allowed me to completely immerse myself in my studies. Well, let's face it, there weren't many distractions. Or maybe it was that I kept myself so busy that I couldn't afford any distractions. I took over twenty hours a semester and participated in every Theater project that I could. Before I knew it, the four years had flown by. I graduated in May of 2001 with my Bachelor of Science degree in Theater and a minor in Rhetoric. I even received Valedictorian honors for my 4.083 GPA. But even with all my education, I still didn't have a clue how to get started on my career in acting.

CHAPTER 4

JUST A GENERAL HOSPITAL

I had always felt drawn to Hollywood, but I didn't know how to make that leap from dreaming to reality. It's funny, but when you grow up in a remote area and have no money, it's almost *impossible* to believe that you can just up and move halfway across the country to a huge city. I had never been to California before, and I didn't know anyone who lived there. It took about a year after I graduated college to make the move to LA and it was a difficult process.

After graduation, I took the summer off, and then ended up following my boyfriend (from college) to Urbana, Illinois, where he was attending graduate school. When I arrived in town, I opened up the local paper and checked the Want Ads. At first, I got a job at a movie theater as a ticket taker. (Yes, my Theater degree was really coming in handy.) I stood beside the sixteen year old stoners behind the counter and tried not to commit suicide.

After a few days of minimum wage embarrassment, I opened up the paper again and gravitated towards the largest ad— the local hospital, (the biggest employer in the city.) I brought in my resume to their Human Resources Department and got a job working forty hours a week as a MAA (Medical Administrative Assistant a.k.a. Secretary). I felt really lucky to be hired. After all, I was making $8.37 an hour, more than I had ever made in my entire life! I worked in the Rheumatology, Physical Medicine, and Psychology Department.

I was excited to start working, but after four years of college, it was strange to be thrust into the real world. I had grown quite comfortable studying Shakespeare, learning the structure of the Globe Theater, and pulling "all nighters" critiquing 18th Century Restoration Literature. I had spent four years developing these skills. Honing them. Fine tuning the art of being a student. But when I showed up at the hospital for my first day, I quickly got a dose of reality.

I remember thinking, "I'm here. So where's my quiz? I found myself wondering, "What will my term paper topic be this quarter? When are the dates for Spring Break this year? I need to mark them on my calendar. How many more hours do I have left until I..." Until I realized; I *had* graduated. I *had* completed my 120 plus course hours. I had already finished all of my quizzes. My term papers had all long been handed in and graded. There were no Spring Breaks anymore. No need to mark a calendar. I had nothing to plan. And unlike my college years, I had no guide. No list. No directions. Nothing.

All I had to do was show up five days a week at 8 a.m. and leave when they turned the lights off, or when I heard the vacuum start up down the hall. I had only to remember to answer the phone, "Carle Clinic West 3 this is April," and to do my best to locate the patients in the computer by using their last name, not their Social Security number, (because corporate thought it gave the nice illusion of personability.) Oh, and to not forget to collect the co-pay. And I could do all of this. I could do all of this pretty well, because I was used to working hard and following orders. But I was unfulfilled.

The hospital definitely had an interesting mix of patients, nurses, and doctors. But I kept having the haunting feeling that I was living someone else's life. It was like I was a character in a sitcom, always on cue, but never hearing the laugh track. The work was very tough, but probably only typical of an office job: where the women are overworked and underpaid, where you have to stand on your feet all day long, and where the Dr. Shoals cushioned comfort old lady shoes just won't cut it. (To give you an idea of how badly my feet hurt after I finished my first day, as exhausted as I was; I actually went to Wal-Mart specifically to buy a pair of those nursing shoes with the thick soles. Something that I thought I would never do, and I wore them every single day until the day that I left!)

I remember wondering, "How can women stand on their feet all day long like this? How can they be expected to answer so many phone calls? There was hardly enough time to go to the bathroom or barely pop two Advils, and there were no "coffee breaks." No, this was no office sitcom. There were no silly hijinks. It was like we were a randomly selected group of people trapped on a boat together steered by a blind Captain. We were racing ahead at full speed, but at the end of the day we were back where we started. And we had no choice but to make the best of it.

I can't remember the statistics, but an independent survey

group had observed our department and recommended, based on the amount of patients we had and the phone call volume, that we should have at least six secretaries working at all times. But, of course, we had two. Just me and another girl, who was dating a guy in jail, from what I recall. On Thursday afternoons, we would get a temp, a woman who would help us out for three hours. She was in her mid sixties, short, with thick dark hair and a thicker British accent. She was long retired, but liked to get out of the house. She was the one person who actually wanted to be there, and she was usually smiling. I tried to smile too. I did my best, but it was hard.

I survived eight months in this incarceration. Until, so miserable inside, I couldn't take it anymore. I felt like my life was passing me by. I remember working through the winter months— I never saw the sunshine. I was getting to work, before the sun had come up. And I was getting out of work, after the sun had gone down. I felt trapped in this large concrete building. It was a world unto itself. And it was easy to forget those on the outside. After a couple of months, I too was an insider. And I watched the other insiders come and go. Women with husbands and children and mortgages. Women who *had* to work. I sat beside them at lunchtime in the lounge as I ate Lunchables and watched Soap Operas (Soap Operas became the highlight of my day). I watched the Doctors happily hustle and bustle (happy because they were actually making money.) Yes, every two weeks they would give me a paycheck, but they would also take a little piece of my soul.

I was only an ant. And I knew that I was only an ant. I would quietly do my job during the day, and then come home at night, turn on my cheap halogen lamp, and listen to records of

Johnny Cash. I would sit on the floor of my sparsely decorated apartment and paint acrylic portraits of abstract figures. Figures that were jumping, figures that were walking up stairs, figures that were standing amidst tall, towering, dark city buildings. Figures that didn't have faces, but had purpose. I had a face, but I needed a purpose, too.

After I would get off work, I would drive to the local PBS station and volunteer to run camera for the Telethons. Yes, as you can imagine, it was really exciting. Okay, maybe not, but the girl who taught me how to use the camera was studying film at the local college. And after about five minutes of her instructions on wide shots, medium shots, and close ups, I asked her if she wanted to move to Los Angeles with me. She definitely thought that was a strange question, and she looked at me kinda funny. But I told her I was serious, and I gave her my phone number.

A few weeks later, I read about some student film auditions on the PBS bulletin board. I auditioned and was cast in one of the projects. When I showed up for my first day of filming; guess who was running camera? Yes, that *very* same girl! By this point, I knew it was fate. And I reminded her again of my earlier proposal.

Two months later, she called me up and asked if I was still serious about LA. I told her that I was, and that I could give my notice tomorrow. She said that she was graduating in two weeks, and that she didn't really have a plan; but she would get back to me. Excitedly, I hung up the phone. After a couple of minutes, it rang again. I quickly answered it, and I heard only two words, "I'm in."

The next day, I went back to the hospital and gave my

two weeks notice. I felt almost silly explaining my situation to my boss. "Um, I'm actually leaving because I'm moving to Hollywood to try to become a movie star..." I'm sure that my Office Manager hadn't heard that one before. When the Doctors got word that I was leaving, they each wished me luck. Most were supportive. But I remember one of the older Doctors telling me that LA was urban and ugly, and that I would hate it and be back working in the hospital in no time. I tried to smile, but I really wanted to tell him to kiss off. But— I was raised better than that. So, I kept my mouth shut and thought to myself, "He doesn't know me. Once I get to LA, I'm *never* coming back!"

And two weeks later, I printed off Mapquest directions to Los Angeles, got a bacon, egg, and cheese biscuit from McDonalds, and headed west.

CHAPTER 5

CALIFORNIA HERE I COME

I had never been to California before, and *man* it was a long drive! I drove my Chevy Blazer across our very vast country for three days, (while my new found friend followed behind in an old minivan). When we got about an hour outside of LA, my Mapquest directions gave out, and I signaled to exit. I had never seen such large highways in all of my life, and the sea of cars almost gave me a panic attack. I was thanking my lucky stars that it was rush hour and that everyone was bumper to bumper and only going ten miles an hour. Otherwise, I was certain that I would have wrecked myself.

After a few days in economy hotels, we rented a 600 ft. studio apartment in downtown Los Angeles for 700 dollars a month (plus deposit). We ended up being totally scammed by the Middle Eastern manager. He told us that the apartment available was currently being "remodeled,"and that he couldn't actually

31

"show" it to us. (Which come to think of it, should have been a bright red flag, but it was the cheapest apartment that we could find, and we were very naive.) But, on the bright side, he told us that we would be able to choose the color of the carpets and the paint for the walls. And that pretty much sold us. (After much consideration, we excitedly picked out purple!) He explained that our apartment was wired for cable, and that we had Ethernet throughout the building. (It ended up not even having a phone jack or a working oven.) He convinced us that downtown was the best place to live in LA, and that it was very safe and close to everything! (For those of you familiar with LA, it was off of Figueroa and Venice on a nice cul-de-sac underneath an overpass behind the LA Convention Center. So our backyard was a razor wired fence.) Yeah, we should have done a little research...

When we excitedly unlocked the door to our new cool purple pad, we found the walls white and the carpet brown. Confused, we mentioned the error. Our manager seemed just as *surprised* as we were and blamed his Spanish speaking handymen for the mistake. Yes, our lovely home sweet crackhouse. But every downside has an upside. The hot water didn't work, but it did have two prostitutes working upstairs!

We spent the next couple of weeks making practical business moves like buying twin mattresses and a dresser from the Salvation Army Thrift Store. We would circle around the streets of downtown LA trying to find groceries or a gas station like two blind turkeys. She was usually driving, and I would do my part by unfolding and refolding our large city map. Everything was so confusing and difficult. We had to try to locate a phonebook to find Internet providers. Then, we had to wait for an appointment. When a technician finally showed up, we realized that we couldn't install the Internet, because we didn't have a working phone jack. No, it had been painted over during our apartment's major "remodeling." We had to beg for a phone jack to be installed and that took time. We were clueless. I purchased a large book with the listings of Los Angeles acting agencies and started printing off headshots and resumes from my computer and mailing them out in bulk. I included the following cover letter in the envelopes:

Dear Talent Agency,

L.A. is fun. I've been here three days now and although it's a long way from the peach trees of Missouri, I'm beginning to feel right at home in my downtown apartment. The manager said that the neighborhood is so safe, with the barbed wire fencing and the guard dogs and all, that he'd even let his sister live here. And all of my Spanish speaking neighbors seem to agree (though I'm really not sure). Everyone here is so nice—especially the men. I must admit all their attention makes me feel like a real star! I never knew how kindhearted people could be: helping me carry in my groceries, carrying in a heavy dresser my roommate and I bought from Discount Furniture and Meats, and even giving me a quick lesson on the Spanish language (did you know that Puenta Ave. is not pronounced the way you might think?)

Anyway, I've sent my headshots out to several independent and student films and have already received several offers. Unfortunately, since I'm not interested in soft porn at this time, I haven't actually auditioned for anything as of yet; but I'm optimistic. I know I'll be a big success, and it's just up to which one of you will be the lucky one to snatch me up first. I look forward to hearing from you and thank you for your time.

Sincerely,
April

While I waited to hear back from an acting agent, we continued exploring our new city. We consulted a travel guide to LA and read about Sunset Blvd. and the *Viper Room, Whiskey a Go Go*, and *The Key Club*. (Those were clubs where great groups like "The Doors" used to perform.) One night, we decided to check them out. We drove for a half hour and found the busy Sunset Strip filled with cars, neon lights, and people. We tried desperately to find parking, but all the metered spots were taken. (You have to pay for parking everywhere in LA.) We had to pay twenty dollars just to park in a lot. (So there went half of our budget for the evening.)

We got to the doors of the clubs and realized that you had to pay a cover charge just to get inside. It was fifteen bucks per person, and we didn't have enough cash. There were lines all along the sidewalk in front of some of the clubs, and we really wanted to go in and take a look. One doorman actually let us in for free, but once we got inside; we were smacked with disappointment. The clubs were filled with, what looked like, a lot of 1980's rock band wannabees—and not in a good way. Everyone looked like they were trying way too hard to look cool. I quickly discovered that those clubs were long past their hay day, and it was a real let down. We decided to leave the club and just walk down the sidewalks instead. We passed by two men that looked familiar to me with a busty blonde sandwiched in between them. As they passed us on the sidewalk, I tried to recall how I recognized them. (It ended up being Cato Kalin and Bill Maher.) We couldn't figure out who they were at the time, but we were excited. We had seen our first famous people, perhaps this town was going to be exciting after all!

About an hour later, we ran into two twenty-somethin'

guys on the street, and they started to talk to us. They seemed nice, and we exchanged numbers. Thankfully, they were good guys. (I actually ended up dating one of them for a year after that.) The following week, he called me up one afternoon and invited me to go to a Beverly Hills "Gumbo Party." I double checked to make sure that it was *soup* he was talking about, and not short for some strange "couples club" or anything. (You never can be too careful). He reassured me, and said it was like a BBQ. So, I gave him my apartment address, and he told me he would pick me up around seven. I was excited and decided that I needed to buy a new outfit to wear. I persuaded my roommate to walk downtown with me to do some shopping. We came across a store on Broadway St. called, "The Five Dollar Store." I remember thinking, "Slightly unimaginative, but to the point." We walked inside, and I was delighted. It was filled with thousands of wo-mens' shirts and most everything was five bucks! Since I didn't have much money; this store was *heaven*. I must have bought ten tops! There wasn't a dressing room, but I had a good eye for what would fit me. I also found a stretchy short denim dress inside for fifteen bucks. It was a little more expensive, (compared to my shirts), and I was hesitant. But I thought it would be perfect for the party, and I really wanted to make a good impression.

We walked home, and I quickly got ready. I paired the dress with some new flip flops that I had recently bought from Payless, and I switched over my purse to a small denim one that matched perfectly—well, almost perfectly. The denim was a *little* lighter. (It's so difficult to match denim. Isn't it?) But I figured it's a BBQ, or a *Gumbo-Q*. No one will be looking too closely at what I'm wearing anyhow.

Around seven, I got a call on my cellphone. My new guy

friend was lost. He said that his navigation had brought him to the address, but that there must be some mistake. Because, he was on a dead end road downtown underneath an overpass. He started laughing and said, "I got to the barbed wire fence and the trash dumpsters, and I figured I better just give you a call and ask for directions. Before I—" But I cut him off and said, "No, you're here!"

I took a deep breath, grabbed my purse, and walked outside. His new silver BMW was parked in front of the door. I was nervous. Not only had I never been to a Beverly Hills house party before, but I had never been in such an expensive car either. I opened the door and sat down inside. It was immaculately clean and still had that new car smell. As I was checking it out, I noticed that he looked rather pale and uncomfortable. I asked him if he was feeling okay, and he asked me if I actually *lived* in that apartment. I told him that I had just moved in two weeks earlier. He explained to me that this *particular area* was really unsafe to live in, and that he was nervous just driving around there! I shrugged my shoulders and said, "Well, it was the cheapest apartment listed in the newspaper. Besides, it doesn't seem that bad to me, but we are having a little trouble with our hot water." He asked, "Oh? What kind of trouble?" And I said, "Well... we don't actually *have* any." He looked at me kinda strangely and then quickly sped away.

We drove through the beautiful Beverly Hills neighborhood looking for the address. When we slowed down in front of the extravagant house, I began to get nervous. And as we walked up the front walk, I began to feel a little queasy. Maybe I wouldn't fit in. As we opened the front door, my fears were magnified as I watched all the women in the room (all in designer clothes) turn and look at me; just for one shocked and disapproving moment, before they returned to their cocktails and idle chatter. This was no ordinary house party! Everyone was wearing designer dresses, fancy shirts, and high heels! There was a bartender in the corner, and waiters walking around carrying trays of hors d'oeuvres and glasses of wine. And I was in flip flops! I wanted to turn around right there and make a beeline for the Beemer, but I swallowed hard and calmly asked my date, "Okay... So, where's the gumbo?"

The following week, an agent finally called me in for a meeting for potential acting representation! I got the phone call on a Friday afternoon. He wasn't impressed with my "do-it-yourself" headshot, but my cover letter had sparked his interest. He asked me to bring my headshot, resume, and my acting reel to my appointment on Monday. I asked him, "My acting *what*?" He said he needed a VHS tape of all of my movies, Television appearances, etc. He stopped for a second and asked, "You *do* have one... right?" And without hesitation, I said, "Oh, yeah! Of course I do!" After I hung up the phone, I looked at my roommate and asked her if her video camera from college still worked.

That weekend, we filmed four different fake movie scenes for me. Since our neighborhood (in the hood) was so dangerous, we were very limited in our filming locations. We were scared to death to actually leave our apartment building, and so we filmed everything inside of it. We just used different angles. First, I was a spy in a black evening dress pretending to pick the lock on our apartment door. Next, a business woman searching my boyfriend's apartment for "the envelope." (I never did figure out what that was supposed to be...) Then, I was a sexy assassin that had to hide behind a shower curtain and sneak out through the window above the bathtub. Finally, I was a lonely, depressed woman who drowned herself in a bath. (And yes, it was the very same tub.) And no, they weren't Academy Award winning performances. (Maybe made for TV movies at best.) But with each scene we filmed, my resume got longer and longer. I went from zero movie experience to four leading roles! It was a brilliant little system, and we were quite proud of ourselves.

I met with the agent the following week, and after he watched my tape; he signed me on the spot! He was very impressed.

Now, I had an agent. But since I had no recognizable film or TV experience, and because I wasn't union; it was nearly impossible to get any work. It was hard to even get any acting *auditions*, because you have to be SAG just to get in the door. It's really a catch 22 situation. You have to *be* SAG to audition *for* SAG films. Go figure. So, I asked around, "How the heck do you become union?" I learned that in order to become union you had to either be hired directly for a SAG project, (which is called a Taft Hartley,) where basically the film or commercial says that they couldn't find a union actor as good as you for the role (You would be surprised how many Movie Producers use this as a carrot for naive young girls. I've lost count of how many Producers I've come across who promised me lead roles in their movies!), or you can become SAG, a much less glamorous way, from doing background work. That's what I did.

The next few months, I was a full-time, "extra." As in the people walking down the sidewalk behind your favorite stars, or the couple sitting in the booth behind them in a diner. I was paid around sixty dollars for an eight hour day, and it was my bread and butter. The calltimes were extremely early (5:30 or 6:00 a.m.)

and the days would run long (over twelve hours). But it let me pay my rent. After a few months, I earned three SAG vouchers and was eligible to join the union. Once I paid the 1300 dollar membership fee, (or rather, put it on a credit card,) I was given my SAG card. Now, I could finally start auditioning!

After seven months, I realized that acting was a much tougher profession than I had *ever* imagined. I had landed a co-star role on the FX series, "The Shield," a hosting spot on TBS's, "Ripley's Believe It or Not," a JC Penney commercial, a Dunkin Donuts commercial, and a guest star role on, "CSI Miami"; but I was still broke and now sharing a two bedroom apartment with four girls in West Hollywood. So, I decided that I needed to do something else.

I had met a guy at a party who had claimed to be a mod-eling agent, and he had given me his card a couple of months earlier. But, like most guys in LA, I assumed that he was lying and just trying to get a date, so I had thrown it in a drawer and forgot about it. But, one day, I ran across the card and gave him a call. It turns out, he was legit. He really did work for a modeling agency.

I never really believed that I could be a model. I grew up looking through YM, Teen, and Seventeen Magazines *wishing* that I could be a model, but since I was only 5'6," I didn't think it was possible. I was always under the impression that models were all six foot tall (or at least 5'9" according to all the magazines.) FYI, all models lie about their height. (So, all those supermodels never really were 5'11" to begin with; they were really 5'9." And all the 5'9" girls were really 5'7," and all the 5'7" girls were really 5'4.") Anyway, I didn't think that I was tall enough, so I never really gave modeling much consideration. But I was tired of being broke and decided to take a chance.

I met with the agent and two women at the agency, and they signed me! However, I had no previous modeling experience, and therefore, no modeling photos. And the first thing you have to do to get work as a model is build your portfolio (book of photos that you show clients during a casting). Of course, if you have never had a modeling job, it's hard to have photos. That's the Catch 22 of starting out as a model. But a good agency will help you get started by setting up "test shoots."

A "test" is basically a photo shoot where the photographer, makeup artist, clothing stylist, and model all pool their talent and work for free. In exchange for their contribution, everyone gets photos for their portfolios. The thing is that most really good photographers, makeup artists, and clothing stylists are too busy working (and getting paid) to do tests for free. So, you're basically doing photo shoots with people trying to get established in their respective fields; which makes for an interesting stack of sometimes *crazy*, and sometimes *hideous* photos, that may or may not be useful to you.

Early on, my agent begged some good photographers to do tests of me. Those photos helped me get my first job— an editorial for Glamour Magazine. (But, to be perfectly honest, I still have no idea how I booked that.) I showed up at the casting only to find a cattle call of 300 models. Amazingly, I was one of three girls chosen for the magazine! My second job was a calendar for Bacardi which paid 2500 dollars for an eight hour day. Then, I did some billboards for Coors that paid 3500 dollars a day. Within a couple of months, I was rolling in dough (or at least compared to how I had been), and life was looking good.

I decided that I would much rather be a working model than a starving actor any day! And not only that— but modeling was fun, exciting, and pretty easy! I continued to do a little acting here and there, but modeling became my focus and continued to be for the next two years.

PART 2

MY DAYS AS # 14

CHAPTER 6

THE AUDITION

It was 7 a.m. on a brisk Thursday morning in October of 2005. I was sitting in a makeup trailer in Hollywood as the artist smothered my lips with a sexy pale pink MAC lipgloss. It was a photo shoot for a new energy drink, and I was cast as the "hot model girlfriend" of a Motocross star. He and I were to pose inside of a convertible that was going to be on top of a trailer that would be pulled down the busy Hollywood Blvd. We were going to have a Police escort and the photography crew was going to hang off the side. Sounded pretty complicated to me, but all I really had to do was look pretty. I slipped on a tight black dress and held out my arms as the Makeup Artist and her Assistant rubbed bronzing lotion all over them and down my legs. I yawned; it was early. And okay... so it wasn't Rocket Science, but hey; I was making a living.

As I walked down the steps of the trailer, I ran into another model friend of mine also booked on the job. We were catching up, and she told me about this gig she had just landed on a new gameshow. She said that they had just finished the pilot episode, and that it had already been picked up by a network. She told me that they were having an audition to replace one of the models and that I should go check it out. It had been a long time since I had been on TV, and I was intrigued. I got the name of the show, called up the casting people, and scheduled an appointment.

A few days later, I arrived at a studio in Hollywood wearing what they had instructed me to: a short skirt, high heels, and a bikini underneath my clothes. I walked into a lobby filled with around fifty models. I muttered to myself, "Great! A cattle call." I had a Poloroid taken and filled out an information sheet.

When it was my turn, I walked into a room along with two other girls. Two male Producers, and a female Wardrobe Stylist were sitting behind a table. A camera guy was filming the audition. They had us introduce ourselves, and then they asked each of us a few basic questions. Then, we stripped down to our bikinis and walked across the room. We had to walk towards them, do a turn, and walk back (similar to walking a runway). After that, they handed me a Samsonite briefcase and asked me to smile to the camera as I opened it and looked inside. They then asked me to do it once again; but this time to open it and look "sad." I didn't yet know the premise of the show, but I was thinking to myself, "*Yeah,* I think I can open a suitcase..."

After I left, I really didn't expect to get a phone call, since there were so many girls auditioning and only one spot; but, a couple of days later, I did.

CHAPTER 7

THE FITTING

I got a call to come in and meet with the Wardrobe Team to see if I could fit into some dresses that they had already altered for the girl who was being replaced on the show. Once again, they told me to wear a miniskirt, heels, and bring a bikini.

I walked into the studio expecting to be the only model there; but I found four other brunette models in the waiting room. Each of us were called in to try on the exact same dresses. After we tried on each dress, (six to be exact) they photographed us with a digital camera. Then, we had to change back into our clothes and meet with two of the show's Producers. One whom I recognized from the earlier audition; the other one I hadn't seen before. They looked me up and down and asked me a few questions. Then, they asked me to strip down into my bikini. I quickly did; and once again, they looked me up and down. I was beginning to see the pattern here. The wardrobe girls had whispered to me while I was dressing that since I had big breasts that the Producers would *love* me. I had laughed earlier, but now, I was beginning to wonder if they weren't being serious.

It was three weeks before I heard from anyone from the show. When the Assistant Model Coordinator called me, she explained that I had been too tall to fit into the other girl's dresses, and that they had hired a petite model to replace her for the first six shows. But they wanted *me* to be her permanent replacement. I quickly accepted the job. I was thrilled!

CHAPTER 8

"IS THIS A DRESSING ROOM OR A DUNGEON?"

It was my first day as a *Deal or No Deal* model, and I was excited. I pulled into the Sunset Gower Hollywood studio lot, parked my car, and walked over to the soundstage. I was energetic and a little early.

I saw a piece of paper taped to the door that read, "Models Upstairs," with an arrow pointing to a stairwell. As I started up the stairs, I noticed that the gray carpet on the steps was old, worn, and heavily stained. It looked like someone had carried a drippy garbage bag down it several times. It made me cringe. I climbed up two flights of stairs and walked through a door. The room was dark and looked like a sewing area for the Wardrobe Stylists.

I trudged up two more flights of stairs, following the stained carpet up and out through another door, and passed a large black rubber garbage can. I wondered if that was the messy culprit. Black plastic sheets hung down on either side of me hiding what I guessed to be a storage area of some sort. I could see a metal chain linked fence behind it. I walked in further, rounded a corner, and saw a large dimly lit room with a long table in the center. The ceilings were over thirty feet high, and the walls were bare, solid cement blocks. It was the old building's attic. I could see my breath as I stepped closer. I thought to myself, "This *couldn't* be where they were keeping us? Could it?"

Confused, I started to turn around, just as two other models walked through the door behind me. They were carrying paper plates of scrambled eggs, bacon, and fruit. They greeted me quietly as they took seats on the folding chairs. I found myself asking aloud, "Is this our holding area?" They nodded their heads. I was in shock. I said, "It's freezing in here and there are no windows!" "And there's no heat either." One of the girls muttered between bites. She continued, "The food is outside at Stage Six. You better get something quick before hair and makeup." I thanked her and then walked down the dirty stairs to find breakfast. I tried to think rationally. Surely, this is something temporary. Surely, they won't actually make us stay up here for long. But they did.

Weeks passed, but they did nothing to make the conditions more tolerable. We used to refer to our holding area as, "The Dungeon," because of the darkness and concrete walls. And it was always freezing! The temperature in that room would drop below fifty degrees. The girls were shivering; myself included. I couldn't hardly take being that cold. This was where we would eat our breakfast when we arrived in the morning. This was where we would sit for three hours until the shows would start. Yes, this was where we would have to strip down, change into our dresses, and eat lunch. Unless we were having our hair and makeup done or filming, this is where we would stay—and freeze!

We complained to the Model Coordinator, who would always wear a long sleeved winter coat and a scarf while she was up there. I am not even exaggerating! We complained to the Producers. We complained to everyone, and everyone ignored us. But we kept complaining about how insanely cold the room was, and finally; they said they would bring in heaters for us the following day. Guess what they brought? Two beat up wall radiators from the 1950's that wouldn't have heated up a Kleenex box! And one of the heaters was completely broken! We complained again that this was inhumane conditions, and that we were going to get sick from being so cold. But they did nothing for us.

They kept promising they would try to track down some other heaters to correct the problem, but they never did. I was tempted to bring in my own space heater and lug it up the stairs to our little attic hell. But, like most of the girls, I kept thinking that one day I would arrive at 6 a.m. and it would be warm. I kept believing that they *had* to do something. I mean— wasn't this a union show? And as union members aren't we entitled to a comfortable holding area? We should have been.

But we never got any heaters. Instead, we all dressed in layers and brought blankets every day. Eventually, I realized that nothing would ever be done. I began to accept the cold, and I began to accept myself for who I was— just a woman working in a man's world. Suddenly, it was like I was back working in the hospital again. Yes, this time it was a Television Studio, but the rules were the same. I just needed to stand there, keep my opinions to myself, and keep my mouth shut. In this world, I had no say, no voice, and no power. And if I complained, stepped up, or spoke out of turn; I would have no job. So, I kept coming back, day after day with my blanket; trying to put on a smile, and trying to convince myself that all of this was acceptable.

CHAPTER 9

"LINES FOR MAKEUP AND HAIR? OH MY!"

Every morning at 7 a.m. half of the models would be called downstairs into hair and makeup. The other half would follow thirty minutes later. Once you arrived at the hair and makeup rooms, you would be required to sit outside in the hallway in a row of folding chairs and wait...and wait...and wait some more, until it was your turn. Oftentimes, there would be ten or fifteen sleepy and heavily annoyed girls standing in line in the hallway (because they never brought in enough chairs for us). It was a weird, disorganized system. Very hurry up and wait.

As you have probably noticed, the models on *Deal or No Deal* have a distinctive look. (Granted they are all dressed in identical dresses and are obviously going to appear similar to one another, but there is more to it than that.) Each model has her hair and makeup professionally done by a group of Makeup

Artists before each show. There are only two color palettes. One for blondes, and one for the brunettes. They want to accentuate the individual girls as much as possible, but they want to keep them looking very uniform.

When I was on the show, they used eye shadow palettes from Physicians Formula in Baked Gingersnap and Baked Spices on me. Those were three shadow kits that could be used dry or wet. They used a lighter set for the blondes. The artists would also line our eyes with black shadow and put on fake eyelashes. It was actually pretty ironic. The Makeup Coordinator would talk about ordering false lashes for us in *bulk* to save money, but she would still require us to bring back our old lashes to reuse them for the next shoot day. Or another words, we would use the same lashes *twice*. She used to make such a fuss about it. I was scared of her, so I always tried to remember. I would rip off my lashes at night and leave them by the sink, so I wouldn't forget them in the morning. Then, I would bring the dirty lashes, still clumped with mascara and lash glue, and hand them back to her in the morning. And she would pile on more glue and stick them back on me again. It was pretty disgusting. I had never worked a modeling job before where they asked us to *reuse* our lashes. I often wondered how the show could give away millions of dollars, but couldn't afford to let the models have a fresh pair of fifty cent lashes each day?

The makeup for the show was applied pretty heavily to stand up under the stage lights. I often thought we looked like a bunch of Drag Queens backstage, but we looked fine on camera. The main thing I can say about the makeup look is that it is neutral and polished. It was pretty straightforward. Everyone basically got the same treatment: foundation, powder, eye shadow, blush, and lips. All of the models were pretty content with their makeup. But hair, on the other hand, was a totally different story.

Models and hair. Who could have known it would cause so much drama? I guess I was pretty laid back about it. I just sat down in the chair and let them curl, tease, and spray until they were happy. I figured; I was getting a paycheck, so they could do what they wanted. But a lot of the girls were not nearly so relaxed.

No, I remember several crying fits and panic episodes. It seemed that a lot of the girls wanted their hairstyles to reflect their personal preferences, and they were very verbal about it. The Producers, (a couple of middle-aged men) had their own ideas of what style was, (or what they *thought* it was). And since they were writing the paychecks; they had the final decision on hair.

At the beginning of the season, each girl would have her hair done by the stylists, and then go in front of the Producers for inspection. We would be looked over, whispered about, and then allowed to leave. Then, the stylists would sit us down, once again, and tweak us. Sometimes, it was a couple of brushes and a little hairspray. Other times, it meant making a curly hairstyle completely straight or vice versa. Usually, it meant making a cool hairstyle look dated and uncool. After our hairstyle had been "approved," we would be photographed for the, "Model Chart."

The Model Chart was a large piece of cardboard with photos of each of the models on it with our approved hairstyle and makeup look. Each day, before we could leave the Hair and Makeup room, we would have to be inspected by the head Makeup Coordinator. She would scrutinize our hair and makeup and compare it with our photo on the chart. If we were satisfactory, she would mark us off her list. If not, we would be sent back into a chair with directions.

Like I said earlier, in the beginning, I didn't give too much thought about my approved hairstyle. That is, until my hair started to get fried and break off from all the hairdryers and hot curling irons. After a couple of months, I had to cut three inches off my hair because it had been so abused.

By Season Two, I was adamant on protecting my hair from all those hellish styling tools at all costs. I noticed that a few of the black girls wore hairpieces. As I would sit in the chair and smell my hair burning, I would watch another stylist slip a wig on a girl, give it a little fluff, and off she would go. I thought to myself— what a fabulous idea! And I figured if those girls could wear them; then so could I.

I took a trip to a large wig store on Wilshire Blvd in LA and searched for my *Deal or No Deal* hairstyle. You know how a lot of wigs look kinda 1990's. I'm not really sure why that is, but you know what I'm talking about. Wigs that scream country music singer from Texas. Anyway, I picked out a wig that looked like that, (which was basically the way that they fixed my hair everyday for the show anyway) and I took it to the counter.

On the first day back, I slipped it to the Hairstylist (who looked at me with a puzzled look, because I wasn't black). But I just smiled, sat down, and crossed my fingers that the Producers wouldn't notice my synthetic shag. I won't say that it looked wonderful. It didn't. It was kinda stringy, kinda frizzy, and kinda dated, but, then again, it only cost me a couple of hundred bucks. And I wore it for the next eight episodes until I left the show. When I finally took it off, my real hair (hiding underneath) thanked me.

CHAPTER 10

"CAN YOU HEM ME NOW?"

Deal or No Deal dresses: they kinda reminded me of prom dresses on meth. They started off looking normal, but by the time that half the season had passed by, there was something strange and slightly abnormal about them that I couldn't quite put my finger on. Oh wait, I know what it was— they were shrinking!

Yes, as the ratings went up, so did the hemlines. And the hemlines kept getting shorter and shorter *and* shorter as the show became more popular. It was really crazy how short the dresses were. We thought it was ridiculous. They were so short that when we walked up the stairs for the Model March, you could see our underwear underneath. The girls on the front row had it especially difficult, because they had the audience sitting directly below them. It became a running joke that the girls on the front row were always flashing them. They complained. But like the rest of us, they were ignored.

I remember that they used to make the dresses so tight

on us, that a few girls actually had the side seams rip when they started walking up the steps for the Model March. The Wardrobe Assistants had to come onstage with a needle and thread and sew the girls "in" the dresses.

Incidentally, a lot of people are curious if we got to keep the dresses from the show. And as you can probably guess, we didn't. A few of the dresses went into storage at the NBC Wardrobe Department to be used on future TV shows. I hear that the rest of them were sold by NBC or auctioned off on Ebay for charity. Of the 38 dresses that the models wore while I was on *Deal or No Deal*, the Producers were so generous as to let us keep— one. And that's only because we all conspired together during the wardrobe fitting and *decided* that we were going to keep it!

It was a purple tank dress with leather pieces on the side. And during the shoot day, one by one, we casually walked up to the Producers and told them just how much we *loved* that dress! I think that they got the hint (by like the twentieth girl). By the end of the day, they had no choice. I can't remember the exact words, but I recall the speech going something like this, "Hello ladies, the calltime tomorrow has been moved two hours earlier to 5 a.m., because we're gonna go ahead and try to squeeze in three episodes instead of two. Oh... and you'll only be getting a thirty minute lunch, so remember to eat really fast...But surprise! We're letting you keep the purple dress!" And we were like, "Golly gee, you're so good to us."

CHAPTER 11

BACKSTAGE WITH A
BRIEFCASE BABE

A half hour before we would start to shoot, we would filter out of the holding area, walk down the stairs, and go backstage. I would always walk down a little early and try to get a blanket. Like I said before, since it was so cold in the holding area and backstage, we all brought our own blankets from home. But the show had larger, thicker blankets backstage. But only about a dozen or so. Everyone would grab for them at the beginning of the show, and they ran out really quickly. (I'm totally not exaggerating when I say how freezing cold it was!) I'm not sure why they didn't buy enough blankets for all of us. Well, I take that back. I heard they *found* the blankets somewhere, so they didn't actually go purchase any.

Once we went backstage, there were 28 director-type chairs set up for us. They were lined up four rows deep, and they were in numerical order. (1-26. There were two extra for the two model alternates.) It was very crowded and cramped, and we had to squeeze through to get to our seat. We would hang our purses on the back of our chairs or try to slide them underneath. Most days, the Wardrobe Coordinator would tell us not to sit down in our dresses. She didn't want them to wrinkle. Most of the time, it wouldn't have made any difference anyway, but we would try to obey her wishes. We all wanted to sit down, but none of us wanted to get yelled at.

There was always a lot of yelling going on backstage. We had a "Model Coordinator," and an, "Assistant Model Co-ordinator," and I don't believe that either of them new just how ridiculous they were to us. They would listen to their headsets and talk over their radios constantly. Then, they would bark out orders to us like we were dogs. Perhaps they were feeling the pressure from above, but that's still no excuse for the way that they treated us. We were yelled at, screamed at, and herded back and forth like cattle. It became a joke among us models, the way that they would carry on. We would often imitate their behavior. For example, instead of politely asking someone sitting right next to us to pass a magazine; we would scream it right in their face.

Yes, we did what we could to make it through. We were tired, freezing, standing for hours in high heels, *and* being yelled at— but, we still tried to make the best of it.

If, God forbid, we needed to go to the restroom while we were backstage. We had to alert one of the two of them. And they were never okay with it. They would always act heavily annoyed and respond with a huff, "Do you really have to go?" (I always thought it absurd that they would question me, a 26 year old woman, to see if I knew for sure whether or not I really needed to go to the bathroom.) After I nodded yes, they would radio for a PA to escort me to the restroom nearest the stage.

He would follow me out of the soundstage, down the hallway, and wait for me right outside the bathroom door. The whole while, he would be in radio contact with the others giving the play by play. "I am walking Number 14 to the restroom right now. I repeat, I have Number 14 in transit." As I was sitting on the toilet, I could still hear him on the other side of the door. "No, she's still in there. No, she's not finished yet. No wait, I think she's washing her hands now." I wanted to kill him! It was so embarrassing. There was absolutely no reason whatsoever why we needed a bathroom escort. We were adults. We were hired professionals, and there is such a thing as giving people their privacy! (After I left the show, one of the models told me that the girls finally complained to the Aftra Union Representative about the bathroom escorts, and I think they were finally ordered to stop them.)

CHAPTER 12

"BOOB CHECK. BOOB CHECK. 1. 2. 1. 2..."

At the beginning of each show, all of us models would line up on the stage with our cases, and the Producers, Wardrobe, and Makeup Coordinators would look us over. They would scrutinize each model and make sure that everything was just right. A couple of times, the Producer didn't like my bangs, for whatever reason, and a Hairstylist was called up onstage to fix them. Oftentimes, we would watch the Producers whisper to the Wardrobe Stylist. Then, a girl would be notified to go backstage, where one of the Wardrobe Assistants would add extra padding to her cleavage. Yes, extra boob pads! That was the one thing that *Deal or No Deal* didn't skimp on.

In fact, each model had her own personal set of bra padding hanging in a bag by her dress every morning. It even had our name written on it. We each had a black strapless padded bra, a silicon push up bra, a set of silicon pasties, a set of petals, and as much padding as we wanted. Some girls would use three or four different types of padding in the dresses. They would have a padded bra, silicon inserts, and padding sewn into the dress. And if that wasn't enough, they would shove more shoulder pads down in there. Yes, a huge emphasis was placed on breast size.

During the fittings, the Wardrobe Team would ask each of us what bra or padding, or combination of both, that we were using for each dress. They would write it down on the tag hanging on top of our dress. Most girls were instructed to use at least two different things. When we were getting dressed before each show, the wardrobe assistants would double check that we used our approved padding. They couldn't have us going on the stage looking small busted!

Since I already had my internal 350 cc's dose of silicone, they never bothered me about my cup size. But one girl who stood near me onstage (she was pretty flat chested) was constantly hassled about her's. They were always padding her up. And practically every day, I would hear her talk about how she was going to get a boob job, just so she didn't have to go through the aggravation anymore. After Season One, she did go under the knife.

A lot of the girls have had breast surgery, and others are getting it all the time. It's definitely not required or suggested by anyone on the show. But the unspoken understanding is: bigger is *definitely* better.

CHAPTER 13

"PARDON ME SIR, BUT I CAN'T FEEL MY FEET."

A typical day on *Deal or No Deal* would start around 7 a.m. with hair and makeup. The first episode would begin filming around 10:30. We would tape for around three hours. Then, we would break for lunch and resume filming around 3 p.m. We would finish around 6:30. A few times, we filmed three episodes on a day. Those days were terribly long and arduous for everyone. (Let me rephrase that.) On those days, we wanted to die!

Since it takes approximately three hours to film one episode, and we filmed two episodes a day; you can only imagine how badly our feet would hurt. We had to stay onstage until our case was selected. (I might add that my case was never quickly called! I was always left standing.) If we were left onstage, we weren't able to walk around during that time. And let me mention that, *standing still* in three or four inch heels for three hours is much more uncomfortable then *walking around* in heels for that same amount of time. Also, because they kept the temperature in the studio so cold, it made our feet feel even worse. My feet would be so cold that they would actually feel numb! One model had to have the Producers call in a medic because she lost all feeling in her feet! They had her sit down backstage. Then, they slowly tried to warm them back up with hot compresses.

One day, some of the Miss USA Pageant Contestants came in and replaced us for one episode. During that show, one of the pageant girls passed out from standing still so long. She dropped her case and almost fell completely off the stage! Those girls had no idea how tough it was to be a *Deal or No Deal* model. (And they were *used* to being onstage in heels!)

Yes, we were troopers. We put up with a lot of pain and still kept a smile on our faces.

CHAPTER 14

MEET THE DOND DIVAS

Most all of the Briefcase Babes on the show are professional models. Which makes sense, considering that modeling agencies are the ones who send the girls to the *Deal or No Deal* auditions in the first place. I heard about the audition from another model, but most girls were hired through their agencies.

Most of the girls also do Television hosting and/or acting. One of the ladies from Season One had her own swimsuit line. One of the alternates wanted to be a R & B singer. Three of the models from Season One used to be Barkers Beauties on, *The Price is Right*. We had one girl who used to be an exotic dancer. (But that information was kept pretty low key.) A lot of the girls have went to college and have degrees. One girl had her degree in Chemistry and went to two years of Medical School before she moved to Los Angeles to become a model. One girl had just completed Law School. One girl was a former

Miss Rhode Island, and another one was a former Miss Oklahoma. Both had competed in the Miss USA Pageant. And a couple were Playboy models. Most of the girls are single with boyfriends. There was one girl on the First Season who was married, but she wasn't hired back for the Second Season. One girl got married before returning for the Second Season. And one girl got married after finishing the Second Season. One of the models has a ten year old girl, but you would never know it by looking at her.

I knew some of the girls, before I started the show, from working together on modeling jobs in Los Angeles. The others, I met for the first time through the show. We all grew closer as we spent more time working together. As with all people, you will get along with some better than others. But I truly respect each and every girl on the show. It was really an interesting mix of intelligent and talented women. I feel fortunate to have become friends with them all. Some of my best friends are girls that I have met on the show.

Most of the time, all of the models got along pretty well. There were lots of arguments, but they were mostly between the models and the Producers. And because of that, we became a pretty tightly knit group of girls. However, a few times, we had World War III break out. It was insane! During the show everyone would be smiling and playing nice, but once they would break for commercials; everyone would start yelling at each other.

I remember one day, a girl from the front row was arguing with a girl from the back row. I was sandwiched in the middle of them! Half the girls took one girl's side, and the other half was against her. They were fighting because the Producers had decided to create an interactive *Deal or No Deal* Game. They wanted to use images and video footage of us for the DVD, and they expected us to basically do it for free. We felt we were being treated unfairly, and we had to call a Television Union Rep from Aftra to come in and help us negotiate a reasonable rate.

All of us models agreed to stick together, and we refused to sign the contract accepting the minimum payment that the Producers were offering us. As long as we all held out, our chances of getting a better deal were increased. However, one weekend, the Producers called a girl from the back row (the ex-exotic dancer), and they secretly asked her to be the model for the DVD game. They would pay her a small fee if she would come in and be filmed opening the briefcases. They knew that she desperately needed the money, and that she would take their offer.

When we all came to work the following week and found out what had happened; we were furious. She had signed the contract. Now our chances of getting any more money for the game were basically over. Half the girls were angry at her, and the other half were just so frustrated with the negotiations that they just wanted to give up and get paid. Ultimately, that's what we did. We figured a little money was better than none at all. But it really wasn't fair.

Aside from that fight, I was truly amazed at how well the models got along with one another. When you work closely with people for long periods of time, you are bound to get on each other's nerves at some point or another; but it really didn't happen that often at all. That's because the girls are truly nice individuals. They are professional and extremely hard working. And even through hardships and difficulties, they retained a positive attitude and remained committed to doing the best job that they could. Even if, they weren't getting the pay or the respect that they deserved.

CHAPTER 15

THE DIRT ON
HOWIE MANDEL

Well, there isn't actually much dirt on Howie, because he has that whole OCD thing where he doesn't shake people's hands. (Okay, maybe that was a lame joke. But seriously…) Howie doesn't shake hands with the contestants or with the models. He's been very candid about it and says he has a fear of germs. It seems kinda strange; but then again, I try to wash my hands after *I* shake hands with people or touch door handles. I mean, who really wants to catch a cold or pick up some other kind of virus? I guess Howie tries to minimize his exposure to germs altogether. So, maybe, he's got it all figured out.

Howie's a really amazing guy. He's super funny, down to earth, and very professional. (When can you honestly say that about a person? But, in *his* case— it's actually true!) And he has been extremely nice to all of the models. He's always kept a positive attitude and usually has a big smile on his face, which could have been quite a challenge. Because, would you believe that for the entire First Season, this *network show* didn't even give him a separate Makeup Room? They made him have his stage makeup put on in the models' Makeup and Hair Room! (Imagine trying to prepare to host your own show in a room with 28 models, and twelve Makeup Artists and Hairdressers jabbering around you. Hairdryers roaring and hairspray fogging up the air. I don't know about you, but it would have made *me* a nervous wreck!) That definitely wasn't a fair situation for Howie to have to deal with, but he really was a great sport about it.

I remember watching him one day, as he was sitting in his makeup chair, as a model walked over to him and told him that her Grandma was a big fan of his. She went on to say that today was her Grandma's birthday. Howie told her to go get her cellphone, and he called her Grandma back in Chicago just to say hello and wish her a Happy Birthday!

People always ask me if Howie knows all of the models' names. For the most part, he does. He has a teleprompter on the wall that flashes each name once their case has been called, but he usually doesn't need to use it. At first, he did. But as the shows progressed, he got really good at remembering all of our names. I think he made an effort to learn everyone's name very quickly, not only to make the show flow more smoothly, but to demonstrate to each of us models that we were important and worthy of respect. We weren't just a suitcase number. We were a person. I can't speak for the other girls, but I greatly appreciated his efforts, and it meant a lot to me.

I really admire Howie's talent, but also his character. In my opinion, he is a *big* reason that the show has been so successful.

CHAPTER 16

"WILL THE REAL DEAL BANKER PLEASE STAND UP?"

Have you ever wondered who the *Deal or No Deal* Banker is? Does he actually talk to Howie on the phone? Does he come up with the bank offers? Well, wonder no more. The "Banker" on *Deal or No Deal* is an actor who is actually paid to sit up in the booth during the show. (I think he surfs the Internet on his laptop.) He's been there since Season One, and he's a really nice guy. He will move around when Howie is "pretending" to talk with him, but he doesn't actually converse with him.

Howie is really on the phone with the Producers. They tell him the offer. FYI, the bank offer is not simply an average of the remaining amounts. From what I was told, it's selected from a range. The Producers can select an amount on the *higher* end of the range, if they are attempting to get the contestant to take the deal and go home. Or, they can offer an amount on the *lower* end of the range, if they determine that they would like the contestant to remain in the game.

(The sad thing about the Banker is that the Producers made him sign a confidentiality agreement stating that he won't tell anyone who he is. So, unlike the *Deal or No Deal* models (who, even though they sometimes aren't compensated that well, at least get publicity for being on the show), he's not allowed to get any press and can't take credit for his contribution. Which, I think, is really sad. He is a part of the show, too. Even if, he is mostly in shadow. And as a performer, he should be allowed to take credit for it.)

CHAPTER 17

IF THESE CASES COULD TALK

There are 26 briefcases in the game of *Deal or No Deal*. In the beginning, each held an amount from one penny to one million dollars (With the exception of the special games where the prize amount increased). As a model, I never cared what amount my case was holding. Most of the models felt the same way. We just hoped that we would be chosen quickly, so we could go offstage and get off our feet. Once we went offstage, we were free to check our cellphones, read a magazine, hit the craft service table, (that's the food) etc... We just had to remain backstage.

I was Number 14, I believe, for 34 episodes. The other four episodes, I was moved into different spots. (I remember that I was Number 19 once.) In the beginning, they maneuvered us around to try to achieve a balanced look. They attempted to evenly disperse the blondes and the different ethnicities. They also placed the tallest girls in the back.

Once the show took off, the Producers were very particular about keeping the same girls in the exact same spots. They wanted the viewer at home to associate the number with a face. They would only move models around when absolutely necessary, e.g. when a model wasn't available for a shoot date or if someone called in sick. When that occurred, one of the two alternate girls would stand in for the absent model. Other times, an outside model would be hired. (Depending upon whether the alternates had similar coloring or features to the model being replaced.) The Producers always tried to bring in a model who looked very similar to the original model, apparently, to minimize the distraction of their absence.

The general consensus, among the models, was that the front row was the best row to be placed in, because you got more camera time. I was always on the far left side, second row from the back. (And yeah, come to think of it, I guess I usually felt pretty neglected up there…).

The models don't know what amount is in their cases, and neither does Howie or any of the Producers. The briefcases are prepped and handled by an outside security firm to ensure that no one at NBC knows what amounts are in them. They come to us in a large locked box that is wheeled backstage once the show begins. Two men unlock it, as the models get in line in numerical order. When it is our turn, we are handed our case and walk up a set of stairs on the left side of the stage. (During Season Two, they actually started taping the cases shut with masking tape to help prevent a case from accidentally opening should a model drop it as she goes up the stairs. The Stagehands would remove the tape before the cameras started to roll.)

Once we got onstage, we placed our cases on our clear plastic stands and prepared to film some "pick up shots" for the show. The Stage Manager would count down, "3, 2, Smile!" The audience would applaud as we stood still and did the famous "Briefcase Pose." (Left hand on the left bottom corner and right hand on the handle.)

We stayed in that position and smiled…and smiled…and smiled as the cameras moved around and got their shots. We smiled until our mouths got sore and started to quiver. After what seemed like an eternity, the Stage Manager would say, "Relax." Then a man carrying a steady cam (a large handheld camera) would walk towards the stage, as another man followed behind him holding a bundle of cable. Then, once again, we would hear, "3, 2, Smile!" And we would cheese abnormally large, as the two men walked up and down our rows getting our closeups. After they ran out of cable, they would turn around, and we would hear our Stage Manager say, "Get ready for the Model March." Then we grabbed our cases from off our stands and headed down the stairs to the back of the stage to line up for the March.

While we waited backstage, we would gossip and try to warm ourselves on the stage lights. We would have to wait until the cameras were reset and ready for us. Sometimes, we waited back there for twenty minutes. Sometimes longer. We waited for over an hour before. It sucked because there wasn't anywhere to sit down. They didn't really want us sitting in our dresses anyway, but we didn't usually care. Our shoes were torture to stand in. Any second that we could sit; we usually tried to take advantage of it. Some of us would sit on this flimsy wall that separated the stage lights from the set. (But once a couple of girls sat on it, it got all wobbly and felt like it was getting ready to topple over.) Others sat on the stairs themselves.

During this time, our cases were usually sitting haphazardly somewhere on the floor or on the stairs. They weren't locked, and we could have (hypothetically) opened them and sneaked a peak; but nobody did. There were a couple of Stagehands standing around backstage. (Probably secretly eyeing us to make sure that that didn't happen.) But we could have *still* done it, because it was dark back there.

When we heard loud music begin to play (basically a base beat), we knew that we were ready to start. We quickly hopped up and rushed into our places. The music would stop for a moment, and we would hear Howie's voice over the loudspeaker say, "Ladies, Please." Then, the music would start again, and we would begin to count and ascend the stairs. We all walked on different beats, depending on our row on the stage. It was a regular Broadway dance performance as far as I was concerned. Every girl went on a different beat, off a different step, and with a different leg. I never fully understood what the heck we were all doing. I'm not sure anyone really did. I just knew: start on the second step, left leg, on the third 5, 6, 7, 8. (I guess I would never make it on Broadway.) Well, we weren't the Rocketts, but we did our best as we emerged up and over the stage, proudly holding our cases, and trying not to trip down the steep stairs. A few times, however, a briefcase and a girl went tumbling. Heels have fallen off. A couple of girls would go down in a domino effect. A case would drop. Its lid would fly open, and its amount would be bared to everyone as it slid across the floor. The audience would gasp, and I would try not to laugh. (That is... until, I made perfectly certain that the girl was okay of course).

But the pratfalls had a downside. Once a case had been knocked over or fallen open (whether on or offstage), the show had to restart. All the models had to give their cases back, and they were taken away and resorted. Which meant more time standing onstage in those stupid high heels!

We would do the Model March at least two times at the beginning of each show. The Producers wanted to make sure they got enough footage. The second time, Howie would continue with the show. Since we filmed two episodes each day; that was a minimum of four Model Marches. So, we really got our exercise!

Once the show started, we would stand onstage until the contestant picked our number, and Howie told us, "So and so, open the case." But before we could unlatch it, we had to wait until a large light came on at the top of the ceiling at the far end of the studio. You had to see it out of your peripheral vision, because you were looking down at the contestant at the time. Once it came on, you unlocked your case, opened it, and gave your response. (Depending upon what amount was inside.) Then, you had to wait until the same light began blinking, before you could close your case and exit the stage. One word about the "Fake Out." (Where a girl pretends to be sad, but then reveals a low amount. I'm *sure* you have seen it before.) During Season One, we were notified not to use the above mentioned "technique," unless we had received prior approval from the Producers. They said that it was being "overused."

People often ask me if I have had the million dollars in my case. I have a few times. I've had all kinds of dollar amounts in there, but I lost track a long time ago. However, I *do* remember giving the wrong expression one day when I opened my case!

You know how you give a "happy look" for a small amount and a "sad look" for a large amount. But what you don't know is that it's really hard to see what amount you have in your case as you are opening it, because it is turned at such a harsh angle. I had a major cold one day and was on some serious cold and sinus medication. And I thought my 10,000 was 100,000 dollars (the highest amount left in that particular game). And I gave a *really* sad look. After the show, one of the Producers came up to me and asked me about it. I was like, "Oh, I did? Whoops?" He told me not to screw up again.

Have you ever noticed that some of the models are really animated and are always talking to Howie or to the contestants on the show; while others hardly ever speak? (They just stand there and smile.) Well, no— they're not too scared to talk— it's because they're not wearing a microphone! The show only has six wireless microphones for the 26 models.

At the beginning of the show, six girls are "randomly" selected and wired up. The ones (who have mics) have the opportunity to talk when their case is called. The others, however, must stand dumbly and smile. As the show progresses and models exit the stage, they take their microphones off. Those models then *hand over* those mics to the girls remaining onstage during the commercial breaks! Which basically means more work for the models. Funny, they can give away a million dollars, but they won't buy enough microphones for all twenty six models?

To date, no one has won the million dollars yet, but several people have had that amount in their case. I particularly recall one woman from Season Two. At the beginning of the show (before she selected her case), she told us that she had had a dream the night before in which Jesus sat down beside her on her bed and showed her the number to choose. She chose that case number and started the game. She ended up taking a deal for a little over 200,000 dollars. When they opened her case at the end, it contained the million! Everyone gasped. One of the other models standing beside me was like, "Uh, ya know. If Jesus appeared to *me* in a dream... I think, I would have *kept* the case." I had to agree with her.

CHAPTER 18

AMERICA COMES DOWN WITH DOND FEVER

We had no idea that the show would become such a big hit. In the beginning, we were only guaranteed six episodes at a time. We were told that if those episodes did well in ratings, then NBC would order another six episodes, and we would be called back in to work. The whole first season went like that. We went from week to week, not ever knowing if we would have a job or not. Even after the show became a huge success, it was still up in the air whether or not NBC would continue to order episodes, or if they were going to give the show a break as to not burn it out too quickly. But in the end, they decided that America couldn't get enough of *Deal or No Deal* and lucky for us; we continued to work.

With the popularity of the show came some wonderful opportunities for the models as well. It was really great to be included in *People Magazine's 100 Most Beautiful People* for 2006. It came as a complete shock. The Producers told us that People Magazine was stopping by to snap our photos for the up-coming issue. We quickly had our photos taken and didn't give it much thought. A few weeks later, at the beginning of one of the episodes, Howie said he had a big surprise for us. He turned our attention to the *Deal or No Deal* board, and it was replaced with the People Magazine spread announcing the *Deal or No Deal* models as 26 of the 100 Most Beautiful People for 2006. We were ecstatic! It was a real honor.

I also shot two spreads for MAXIM Magazine as a *Deal or No Deal* model. One was for MAXIM Online and was shot at the Standard Hotel in West Hollywood, CA. The other one was for MAXIM Magazine and was shot at a private airport in Burbank, CA.

Other girls have been asked to do Television appearances on *The Tonight Show, Oprah, Access Hollywood, ET, Extra*, and on local news stations.

Just about all of the models quickly became recognizable out in public. I know I had lots of people recognize me from the show. After working on the show for about a month, I was walking through a casino in Vegas and heard several people call out, "Number 14!" After about a half a dozen times, I suddenly realized that they weren't yelling at a casino game, but to me! It seemed that they couldn't remember my name, but they knew me by my *number*! I had to admit— it was pretty funny. It made me laugh.

Deal or No Deal started to appear everywhere. We had

our own DVD game, slot machines in Vegas, Lotto tickets and billboards. Even though it was difficult at times, it was still great to experience the ride to the top. We were a part of the highest rated show on Television. Nineteen million viewers were tuning in to watch us every night, and that was a wonderful feeling.

CHAPTER 19

SEASON TWO: SATAN WEARS A THREE PIECE SUIT

During Season One, the models signed a release each day that we worked. It was flexible and easy. But Season Two would be different. The first rehearsal was held at a new studio in Culver City, CA. The show had moved locations, and we hoped that this meant a better environment for us. And it was better. We actually had nice dressing rooms with clean carpet and couches! We were thrilled. We had put up with so much back in Hollywood, and it was about time that we got a break.

At the beginning of our rehearsal, we were handed a new contract. In order to work, we were required to sign it. Some girls signed right away. Others of us read the fine print. It had some disturbing new rules for us. It basically asked us to give over our rights. We would be required to do any video promos or promotions without receiving any compensation other than the absolute minimum required by law. This didn't make us particularly happy. We felt like we deserved more.

But the strangest part of the contract was that it made each model exclusive to the show and prevented us from acting or appearing in any other Television shows. That meant saying goodbye to all of our acting careers. It might have made sense, had we been series regulars on a network show where we are being paid 20,000 dollars an episode, but it was completely unfounded in our situation. Most of the models wanted to pursue acting careers. (That's why most of us were in LA to begin with.) But none of us wanted to give up our rights to that degree.

We collectively decided that the contract wasn't fair, and the majority of us refused to sign. We were told that the Producers would make some changes to it and make it less stringent. When we came to work a few days later on the first day of Season Two, we were handed our new contract. And the Producers *had* made it more lenient. It didn't prevent us from appearing in *all* other Television shows. It prevented us from appearing in all of them; but *one*. Yes, they were allowing us to appear on *one* episode of *one* Television show. But only if, they approved it in advance. And only if, it wasn't going to possibly air at the same time as a *Deal or No Deal* episode.

Now granted, it is difficult to book an acting job on a Television series, but it's not *that* difficult. I had already been on four different TV shows at this point. But whether or not a *Deal or No Deal* model was even capable of booking a job like that was irrelevant. It's just simply not fair to ask any model or actress to give up their chances to go after great opportunities like that. It's not fair to ask a group of girls to give up their dreams.

They were being selfish. They were bullying us. They

wanted to control us, and they knew that they could get away with it. They had so many other models to choose from now. Even if we all quit, we could easily be replaced by new models who would sign. We were disposable.

About a dozen girls signed the contract then and there. They were allowed to go downstairs to go into hair and makeup. The rest of us, who weren't so willing, were instructed to stay put. The Model Coordinator told us that if we wanted to work that day, we would have to sign. I didn't believe her. I knew that we were going to film regardless. We were scheduled to shoot for the next three days, and in Hollywood—time is money. I knew that there was a studio audience filing in downstairs at that very moment. There was no way that we weren't filming as usual. I was stoic. A few more girls gave in, but I refused to sign.

After an hour passed, we too were allowed to go into hair and makeup. As we finished getting our dresses on, we were told to go backstage. We filed into our designated rows and took a seat in our chairs. We were told that there was an announcement about to be made. I could hear the studio audience laughing and buzzing. They had no idea what was going on behind the scenes. We were all nervous. My stomach was in knots. Some girls were crying. The girls who *had* signed the contract didn't look worried, but they remained quiet and avoided eye contact with me. I was scared too, but I was defiant. I heard someone whisper that we were all getting fired, and that they had called in replacement models for that day. I thought that was nonsense. They were far too cheap to have replacement models waiting in the wings. I thought, "This is all a bluff. We are getting ready to walk onstage any second now, and there is nothing that they can do to stop us." But, I was wrong. They did stop us.

The Model Coordinator announced that everyone who had signed the contract would be allowed to work that day, and that they should stay where they were seated. The rest of us, who had refused to sign, needed to proceed upstairs into a boardroom for a meeting with the Producers and a team of NBC lawyers. I thought to myself, "Nice move. Yes, what a nice, sneaky move."

As more girls started crying, I watched their carefully applied eye makeup run down their faces. They wanted to work. They didn't want to be fired, but they didn't want to give up their acting careers either.

Like ants, we followed the Model Coordinator single file up the stairs, down a hallway, and into a boardroom. We were nervous and anxious. Our hearts were beating fast, and our mouths were dry. We were busily gathering our thoughts, our facts, and our courage, to professionally lobby our case to the Producers. To the Producers who held our personal fates, futures, and careers in their very hands. To the Producers... who didn't even *bother* to show up.

They had a group of Suits do the talking for them. And the Armanis and the Hugo Bosses explained the situation to the roomful of identical dresses. It was nothing *personal*, just *business*. The Producers deeply cared for *each* and *every* one of us, and they would *absolutely hate* to see any of us go. Afterall, we had been there from the very beginning. We had helped them build the show into the huge success that it had now become! *No, no, no*...they hadn't done this *alone*? No, this was *teamwork*! Isn't that right Number 15?... I, I, I mean...Laura. Look, I know this is an unfortunate circumstance, but I want you to know that we're *all* in this together, and there's no *I* in *PROFIT*!...uh, uh, uh, I mean in *"TEAM."*

Their words were misleading, but their motives were perfectly clear to me. I could practically hear the Producers' instuctions, because I had heard words, so earily similar, echoing in my own head once upon a time, "Try to address the girls by their names, not by their numbers, because it gives the illusion of personability. Oh, and don't forget to collect the contracts..."

And the lawyers were right about one thing. It is true that there is no *I* in "*team*," but there is no *I* in "*tears*" either, but there were tears in most every girl's eyes; as more girls broke down as more contracts were signed.

Finally, there were just five of us left. Everyone was silent. They had whittled us down. Weeded us out. The girls who were left weren't crying anymore. They weren't arguing back. No, they seemed abnormally quiet, and their eyes seemed far away. Perhaps, searching somewhere deep inside themselves. To those of us remaining, this was a matter of principle. This was a matter of freedom. It was about having the right to hold onto a dream. Whether or not, it was ever going to manifest into reality. I was in a slightly better position than the rest, I had just completed my first film (*The Dukes of Hazzard: The Beginning*), but even *I* didn't have any other jobs lined up; and I wasn't guaranteed of any. But I certainly wasn't willing to *give up* my opportunities either.

When the Model Coordinator asked me again if *I* was going to sign, I looked her in the eye and said, "I'm not signing this today, and you can't make me. So, I guess you're going have to fire me or let me go downstairs and start working; because, you're only wasting my time up here."

I think everyone in the room was a little shocked to hear those words come out of my mouth. I think that even I was shocked. This show, these people, and these circumstances had challenged my self respect so severely that it had caused me to withdraw. I had become unusually quiet and reserved. I guess I had thought that my verbal solitude was my protective shell. But it had really become the walls of my tomb; where all of my feelings and opinions were trapped inside with me to die. Even though I had kept quiet for months; now, for the very first time, I finally spoke up. I finally heard my own voice, and I liked the way it sounded.

The Model Coordinator didn't respond as she looked down at her watch. A rather disgusted look swept across her face as she told us to all go downstairs. Yes, just like I thought, they were going to let us work for the next three days without signing any contracts. But we were informed that if we wanted to come back to work on Monday; we had to bring them back signed, or we would be fired.

As I stood onstage during those next three days, a lot of thoughts flooded through my mind. I tried to persuade myself that this job really didn't mean anything to me. It was only a headache and a paycheck. But as I watched the audience applaud, felt the contestants' enthusiasm, and saw the smiling faces of my peers standing in the rows next to me; I couldn't help but feel a little sad. Yes, I was only one of the smiles in a sea of 26. But I was "Number 14." I had my place. (So what that it was in the upper far left corner. Second row from the back). I had been a part of something special. And me and this briefcase had been through so much together. We had shared so much pain, but also experienced so much excitement and joy. Yes, it had been quite a ride, but I knew in my heart that my journey was coming to an end.

As I packed up my bag and folded up my blanket after the final show, I heard the Model Coordinator yell for us to return all of our hairpieces and wigs to the Makeup Room before we left for the weekend. My cheap wig was still bobby pinned to my head. It was itchy and uncomfortable, but I had decided that it was coming with me. Yes, I had decided that I wasn't coming back on Monday, and I didn't want to have to explain myself. I didn't want to talk to anybody or to ask anyone's permission. I didn't want to be told that I couldn't take my wig with me, because it was against the rules, or because the Producers wouldn't like it, or because we'd better ere on the side of caution. (Perhaps I would be returning after I got some rest over the weekend.) Yes, I was all too familiar with the rules and rationalizations of their bizarre power trip worlds.

Yes, I knew that they wouldn't allow me to leave with it, but I also knew that (even though I would never wear this hideous hairpiece again, and even though I was probably going to throw it away or tuck it in a shoe box at the back of a dusty closet shelf) I didn't want to leave *without* it.

So, I left the soundstage and planned my escape route. I knew I had no choice but to walk passed the Makeup Rooms and the Makeup Coordinator. I feared that the nosy woman would catch me. I knew I had to make a break for it. I felt that if I could escape with my wig; I was somehow escaping with my soul. Yes, maybe it seems melodramatic, but to me it was a final defiant act against this reign of tyranny.

As my heart pounded almost out of my chest, I held my breath as I quickly walked past the six separate Makeup Rooms. I prayed silently that I would become invisible: that no one would see me, and that I wouldn't hear my name being yelled. I couldn't stand to have one more person treating me like I was a piece of property. And miraculously, no one caught me!

Once I made it out of the hallway and through a doorway into the lobby of the building, I started to run. I burst through the double glass doors and out onto the pavement. Yes, I was a desperate, haggard woman in a jogging suit and a bad wig, but I had a smile on my face and a sparkle behind my eyes.

About fifteen feet into my freedom, I heard a voice behind me yell, "April!" But I didn't stop. No, I wasn't going to look back. I was free, and they couldn't drag me in again. I kept running until I heard the voice again. This time, I recognized its high pitched twang. It belonged to the (used to be small busted) model who stood near me onstage. As in slow motion, I spun around. She was following behind me and carrying my dark blue fleece blanket. I must have dropped it during my sprint. She looked at me strangely as I ran back over to her to grab it. She must have noticed my wig and the deranged look on my face. Because, as she handed it over, she asked; "Are you okay?" For a moment, I didn't respond. I was too busy peering over her shoulder checking the double doors of the soundstage. I halfway expected to see the Makeup and Model Coordinators, and the Producers beating their fists desperately on the glass on the other side. But they weren't there. I guess; I had out ran them. I breathed a sigh of relief and looked down at the girl and said, "Thanks. See ya around."

But I didn't see her around. I never returned to the show. I refused to sign the contract, and so I lost my place on that stage. I was replaced quickly and easily forgotten. My briefcase got a new owner: another brunette with similar features. My friends on the show missed me, and I missed the show. But we both moved on.

It's been almost a year now, and it's my understanding (from talking to my friends who are still on *Deal or No Deal*) that it's a much more pleasant work environment than before. I've been told that it's like a completely different show, and that I wouldn't even recognize it. There are new Producers, new Model Coordinators, and new everything. Yes, all the models seem to really love it now... or so they say.

I guess, if I had stuck it out, it might have eventually worked itself out after all. I'm happy that I made the decision that I did, but I still encourage other models to audition for the show. It can be a very rewarding experience, and from what I hear now; it's *definitely* a lot easier than what I remember.

CHAPTER 20

LIFE AFTER DEAL

When I quit *Deal or No Deal*, I had no other jobs lined up. I basically wasn't sure if I would be working on *any* projects *any* time soon—or ever, for that matter. In Hollywood, you really never can tell what is going to happen. But I was willing to chance unemployment rather than stay in what I felt to be a degrading environment any longer. So, I took a deep breath and started auditioning.

By December, I had completed three more films: a horror film, *Nitetales,* (with Gary Busey), a comedy, *I Do...I Did,* (in which I played a woman eight months pregnant!), and a thriller called, *Coma,* (with Michael Madsen and George Hamilton.) Each film was very different. Each taught me valuable lessons. Pushing myself to the limit made me aware of my talents *and* my weaknesses.

In January, I began doing the press tour for my role as

Daisy Duke in, *The Dukes of Hazzard: The Beginning.* It was really a fantastic experience. I was interviewed by dozens upon dozens of radio stations, TV shows, and magazines. They would send a limo to pick me up at four a.m. that would drive me to my various appearances each day. The mornings in which I would do radio interviews, I would talk with at least twenty different stations in one sitting. Each interview would last nine minutes, and then I would have a minute break until the next one would start. I would have an interview (let's say) in New York at 5 a.m., Florida at 5:10, South Carolina at 5:20. I remember during my first day at the radio station thinking, "When do I get a bathroom break?" After sitting through like fifteen interviews, I finally signaled to the Sound Engineer that I had to go! As soon as we went off the air, I literally leapt out of the seat and raced down the hall! I had to be back on the air a minute later.

I flew to Nashville to be on a show for CMT. They did an hour long *Behind the Scenes Special* on the making of our film. In Nashville, I was also on a country cooking show called, *Country Fried Flicks,* with Hazel Abernathy. She was amazing and so much fun.

I recently completed another film called, *The Penthouse*, in which I was lucky enough to land the lead female role. In addition to acting, I have continued to model, and I have been on the cover of MAXIM Magazine in the UK, Fitness RX, 944, Sense, Image, Rounder, and Knock Out Magazine (where I shot with two panthers!) I also got to shoot the cover of the 2008 MAXIM Celebrity Calendar.

But all of the acting or modeling is neither here nor there. The main thing is that *everything* that I do now is on my own terms. I have learned to listen to myself. I no longer sit back and let someone else make decisions for me. I speak up, and I step up. I have decided that no amount of fame or money is worth losing your self worth. And I would rather be broke than have my spirit broken.

Through leaving the show, I have also learned that sometimes in order to accomplish what you really want to in life; you must venture out of your comfort zone, go out on an edge, and jump into the unknown.

Sure, you may get beat up a little along the way, but it just might be worth it in the end. Since I have moved to LA, there have been times when I've been absolutely broke, with no money for gas, food, or anything. I have the 99 cent Value Meal Menus to thank for getting me through. At times, I've had no place to live, no job, no cash, and no credit cards that worked. But, never for a moment have I ever thought about leaving. Even in the bleakest times, I never gave up hope. I always believed that everything would turn out okay. I know that it's *this* belief that has got me *this* far.

PART 3

HOW TO GET ON
DEAL OR NO DEAL

CHAPTER 21

HOW TO BECOME A
DEAL OR NO DEAL MODEL

Becoming a *Deal or No Deal* model can definitely be a strong career move. Especially, if you are just getting started modeling. It can catapult a model out of obscurity and into the limelight practically overnight. You can get hired one of two ways: either by coming to an open casting call or by sending in an audition tape to the Casting Director. Models from all across the country send in their comp cards, photos, websites, and resumes. From what the Producers told us, the Casting Directors actually *do* look through each package and view every tape.

But even if your material attracts their attention, you will still (more than likely) be asked to come in to an audition with the Producers in person. And due to the incredible popularity of the show, you can only imagine how many girls apply to become models. The Producers literally have hundreds of applicants to choose from, and they are looking for the best of the best. So, just what characteristics are they searching for in a new model? While no one can predict for sure who they will hire next, understanding the current *Deal or No Deal* models might just give you a leg up on the competition.

First of all, *Deal or No Deal* models are not born; they are created. Each girl on the show has had professional experience modeling, hosting, or acting prior to being hired on the show. They have also lived in Los Angeles and have been exposed to the LA lifestyle: fashion, culture, fads. (Among other things.) Those experiences have shaped and molded them: physically, emotionally, and mentally into the models that you see up on the stage. Another words, they didn't start out looking so fabulous. Nope, that's from years of primping and pruning. You too can have their polished model look with a little know how and a little bit of effort. Even if you are new to modeling or don't live in Los Angeles; it is still possible to become a *Deal or No Deal* model if you become aware of what qualities the Producers are looking for in a briefcase babe.

Okay, let's talk about the physical look. If you have watched the show or checked out the photos of the models on NBC's website (www.nbc.com/Deal_or_No_Deal/models/), then you have a good idea of what it takes to physically look like a *Deal or No Deal* model. (As a side note, you can learn a little about the DOND models on NBC's website, but you can learn a lot more about the current models by Googling their names on the Internet. Most of the models have their own personal websites, and you can see for yourself, the types of work that they have done. If I were applying for the show, I would definitely take a little time to research the current models.)

The models on *Deal or No Deal* are between the ages

of 18 and 35, but they all appear as if they are in their twenties. The Producers are looking for attactive, sexy women that will appeal most to their target demographic. They have determined that women in their early to mid twenties are best for their show. If you fit within that range, then you are in good shape. To be perfectly honest, if you are over thirty it might be more difficult to get hired. But, then again, if you look fantastic, or you have a lot of great experience; anything is possible.

You should also be at a healthy weight. Most of the girls are fairly thin. I'd say their dress sizes range from 2 to a 8. I think four is probably the average. I'm not saying that there are any specific weight requirements. (They don't bring out a scale or anything.) But you have to look good in the dresses, and you probably have noticed that the dresses are pretty skimpy. So you need to be physically fit and toned. But you don't have to be perfect by any means. (FYI, the models wear Spanx underneath the dresses. They are thick pantyhose-like biker shorts that act like a girdle to suck you in. I wore them everyday too when I was on the show, but mainly to help keep myself warm.) Yes, it's true, a lot of things can be hidden underneath a dress, but in the audition, you will (unfortunately) be required to wear a bikini. I guess the Producers need to see exactly what they have to work with, or *maybe,* it's simply because the Producers are men. What man doesn't want to see models in bikinis? Whatever the reason, if you feel that you look good in a bikini, then you shouldn't have any trouble looking great in the dresses with the short hemlines and the plunging necklines...

Which brings us to the next physical feature that you might have noticed sticking out of those DOND dresses— cleav-age. As I have mentioned before, a big emphasis is placed on breasts. If you have a big bust, (whether they are natural or not) it's definitely an asset. However, if you don't; don't worry. If you are hired, they will pad you up nicely. You will be a Pamela Anderson before you know it. In the audition, as I mentioned before, you will have to wear a bikini in front of the Producers. If you are on the smaller side (A cup/B cup), I suggest that you pad your suit with silicone inserts. (We call them chicken cutlets, because they look like uncooked chicken breasts.) They are virtually invisible under almost any bathing suit or bra, and they are fantastic! Many models use them on a daily basis and especially for photo shoots. They come in different styles and sizes. They can give you an extra cup size, great lift, and support. And they're a *great* alternative to plastic surgery.

I have had breast augmentation surgery twice now and it's really been a hassle. If I had known then what I know now, I wouldn't have done it. I would have tried the chicken cutlets first!

While I'm on the topic of plastic surgery, I want to point out that most of the *Deal or No Deal* models have a wholesome, natural look to them. They don't look like Porn Stars or Strippers, (not to knock those professions), but I'm just trying to make it clear that they look *classy*. They aren't covered in tattoos or have dark roots or long fake nails. Okay, they may have a couple of tattoos hidden under Dermablend cover-up, and they may have bleached hair and fake nails; but they *still* look classy. And they don't appear to have had any cosmetic surgery (or at least on their faces). They don't look like they have had obvious nose jobs, cheek implants, or lip injections. They look like beautiful versions of the girl next door. I just wanted to mention that, because I think it's important to stress that the Producers are looking for *natural* beauty. Even though the models are dressed identically, they don't, by any means, look like carbon copies of one other. Each is unique and individual. There is no substitution for natural beauty. So, don't feel like you have to be perfect. You are perfect just the way you are because *you* are *you*. (I know how cliche' that sounds, but it's true.) If there is a particular feature that drives you crazy (for example: your nose is completely out of proportion to your face) then maybe surgery could be a good option. But so many people go overboard in their search for perfection. It often ends up looking unnatural. I think that nine times out of ten; natural is a lot more closer to perfect then you might imagine.

Next, let's talk about height. All of the girls are at least 5'5." If you are any shorter than that, it might be a strike against you. But, then again, there are always exceptions to the rule. I did hear recently that they were looking for girls no shorter than 5'7." A friend of mine (who is 5'3") said it was stopping her from auditioning. But I told her to go anyway.

I told her that I know several girls on the show who are shorter than 5'7," besides, you will be wearing heels! So, don't let height worry you. If you have a great look, and they love you, they aren't going to care how tall you are. I would say that if you are at least 5'5," you should have no problems with height, whatsoever. Just stand up really tall if you are on the shorter side. (I once auditioned for a guest starring role on CSI Miami to play a Supermodel. The Casting Directors almost wouldn't let me in because I wasn't 5'9." (I'm 5'6".) But the Casting Assistant (a nice girl who I think felt sorry for me) let me audition anyway. She just told me the same thing, "Stand up really tall when you audition." Guess what? They had over two hundred girls audition that day, but I got the part! I ended up filming down in Miami for the season premiere episode called, "Blood Brothers." So, I know from personal experience that it really doesn't matter what someone says that they want. Height requirements are just guidelines and *nothing* more. Don't ever let it stop you from doing anything. Especially, becoming a model. (While I'm on the topic...) When I was in Miami filming for CSI, I met Heidi Klum (who had a small part in the show). I absolutely loved her, and I thought for sure that she was six foot tall. In her photos for Victoria's Secret, she looks like a giant! But as I was standing in front of her in the lunch line, I realized that she was only 5'8"! I almost passed out and dropped my chicken salad! It was really a wake up call for me. Most of the models that I have met are usually so much shorter in real life, and I think it's great! It shouldn't matter how tall you are. In photos, as long as you are pretty thin, you will photograph taller anyway. Photographers do a trick where they shoot you from on the ground looking up, and it totally gives the illusion of height.

So, what about skin or hair color? You have probably noticed that there are several different ethnicities among the *Deal or No Deal* models. There are whites, blacks, Asians, Latin, mixed, you name it. So, anything goes. Whatever you are— be proud and say it loud.

(One more note about skin color.) The Producers on *Deal or No Deal* like their models to be tan. When I was on the show, they paid for tanning sessions for us before each show. We weren't required to go, but most of us did. We felt that it made us look better under the heavy stage lights. Most of us spray tanned with Mystic Tan (sunless tanning solution). Sunless tanning creams look really natural now, and you can get dark quickly without damaging your skin. When you are auditioning, I suggest that you get a nice tan. Whether it is real or sunless, a healthy glow will not only make you feel great, but it can also make a night and day difference in how you look in your bikini. Of course, I guess I should mention that too much real sun will age you, could cause skin cancer, and turn your skin to leather. (But I think you know that already.) I'm trying to help you get hired here, so I have to be honest. So, whether it's real or fake, most people look best with a little bit of a tan. I know that I do.

As far as *Deal or No Deal* hair color goes, there are currently fourteen brunettes, ten blondes, and two red heads on the show. At times, the Producers will be looking for a specific type. For example, they recently wanted another brunette and a red head. So, what did they do? They found a blonde that they liked, and had her dye her hair dark. And they found a brunette that they liked, and had her change her hair to red. See, it's all quite illogical.

So, whatever hair color you have is just fine. Just make sure that it looks vibrant and healthy. As far as your hairstyle goes, make sure that it looks clean and professional. I would try to copy some of your favorite DOND models' styles. Find one that works best for you. If you want to wear your hair straight, I would suggest experimenting with a straightening iron to give it a polished look. Remember, your hair shouldn't distract from your face. It should complement it.

"Number 14, open the case." While opening the brief-cases, the models' hands are clearly in focus. So all the models are required to have similar manicures. When you are audition-ing, make sure your hands and feet are nice, and that they have either a French manicure or a neutral, light colored polish (like a nude or a pale pink). Avoid any dark nail colors: red, dark pink, orange, brown, or black. If you are hired, the producers will pay for you to have manicures and pedicures before each set of shows. And remember, you will be filmed opening a briefcase during the audition, so your nails will be highly visible.

I personally like French manicures, but it's nearly impossible to keep them looking good for very long on natural nails. So, I used to get white acrylic tips. Yeah, it damaged my nails a little underneath, but then again; my nails always looked perfect. I didn't have to worry about breaking one or polishing them. I just went in every two to three weeks and got a fill. Now, I have found a new organic product called Calgel that prevents your nails from breaking. It's a clear polish that they simply brush on. (I have it done in a local Japanese Nail Salon.) I think it's pretty hard to find, but it's an amazing product; and I definately suggest it!

In addition to your nails, the way that you do your makeup for the audition is also extremely important. You want to look your very best, but you are also trying to get the Producers to believe that you would fit in nicely with the other models on the show. Therefore, it would probably be best to do your makeup as if you were already on the show. If you take a look at the models' makeup, you will notice that it looks very polished. You should do the same. Before you begin, make sure that you have removed any and all excess facial hair, and that your eyebrows are in tip top shape.

I suggest you start with your eye makeup first, especially if you are working with dark, smoky colors. I learned that tip from professional makeup artists. This way, you clean up any spills under your eyes, *before* you do your foundation. (If you have ever tried to clean up spilt eyeshadow under your eyes, only to have it smear all over your face; you will understand why.) As far as eye makeup goes, you need to play up your eyes with shadow, (using at least three colors: lid color, contour, and highlight). I find that buying a good makeup brush set for your eyes really helps with shadow application. I bought a set from MAC, and it changed my life! I was all thumbs before, but now I love to use eye shadows. I also highly recommend MAC shadows, because they are highly pigmented and a little goes a long way. One pot lasts me for years. Also, their colors are really beautiful, and they are the favorite of most professional Makeup Artists. You should also use a black eyeliner, or use an eyeshadow brush to apply black shadow as liner. (I use a small flat brush from MAC, and it works great.) I find that it is a lot easier than using eyeliner. And black really makes your eyes stand out. You can also use an automatic black pencil liner on the inside of your bottom lid. Lining the inside of your bottom lid really makes your eyes pop. It looks really dramatic and beautiful. I would also curl your lashes and use lots of mascara or wear false lashes. But try to keep it all looking clean and natural. After completing your eyes, clean up any spills, put on a little moisturizer, and move on to foundation.

I have found a great way to apply foundation! It's by using a large, thick, dense makeup brush called a, "buffer brush." It reminds me of a man's shaving cream brush, but it has a blunt, flat end. MAC has some available. You pour some liquid foundation onto a small plate or mirror and dip the brush in it. Then you brush it all over your face. Don't be afraid to really brush it all around. Make sure you get in rubbed in firmly around your nose. You will be amazed at how fabulous it looks! It gives you a professional airbrushed look at home, and it is so quick and effortless.

If you have areas that need more coverage, just apply more foundation. The brush allows you to layer it perfectly, and layering allows you to get great coverage, but still look natural. I would definitely suggest investing in this kind of brush. It is a miracle worker!

After foundation, apply concealer if you need to brighten up under your eyes or cover any blemishes. Then, move on to blush and/ or bronzer. I would use a large fluffy brush to apply them. Avoid using those tiny brushes that come with blush kits, unless you are taking it with you for touchups. Smile, and apply blush to the apple of your cheek, sweeping upwards towards your temple. If you are applying a powder bronzer, you can lightly sweep it on your cheeks, forehead, chin, and nose. Remember to start with a little, and then layer if you want a heavier look. If your skin feels oily at this point, you can add a little loose or pressed powder to help set your makeup. If your blush looks a little dull after applying powder, brush on another light layer to bump it up.

When it comes to lips, I would stick with neutral colors, and use a light colored lipstick or lipgloss. (Dark colors come across as too harsh or heavy.) If you want, you can begin by lining your lips with a neutral pencil. But make sure it's the same shade as your lips, so that you don't have a dark line. I am a big fan of MAC lip glosses called Lipglass. (One of my favorite colors is PRRR.) They are beautiful colors: glossy and very glamorous. And they are a favorite of professional Makeup Artists.

I have seen some of the recent model casting calls, and they seem pretty hardcore. You can watch a few of them on the

Internet on *You Tube*, and some on the DOND website. Girls have to stand in line for a long time. Sometimes, they are outside in the heat. It might be difficult to look your best under those circumstances, but you need to try. You should reapply pressed powder and lipgloss right before your audition to make sure you look fresh. I would also bring a brush and hairspray in my purse for touch ups if necessary.

Oh, and one more thing— your smile. *Deal or No Deal* models are famous for their smiles. It is similar to a beauty pageant smile. Big, but friendly and relaxed. If you've got a great smile—fantastic! If you're not a big "smiler"…then get to practicing in that mirror.

Okay, now let's be completely realistic here. If you're not a model, or you don't at least *look* like a model, then you might not be a good candidate for a Briefcase Babe. You have to have a physical look that fits in with the other models on the show. You wouldn't try out to be a heavyweight boxer if you were 5'1" and 95 pounds, because you would understand that you aren't right for the position. The same thing goes for auditioning for a *Deal or No Deal* model. You have to have the appropriate look. That means, you look somewhat similar to a typical fashion or beauty model. Do you feel like you could blend in among the briefcases? If so— you probably can! So, now that you've got the physical stuff sorted out, let's examine what other characteristics the models have in common.

Each of the models on DOND lived in Los Angeles before they were hired. There are technical reasons for this: the auditions are held in LA (therefore, most girls that attend the auditions live here), and the Producers continue to hire local girls (because they need the model to be ready to start work immediately, if necessary). They need a girl who is ready, willing, and able to focus all of their attention on learning the ropes on the show. A Producer probably won't want to hire a person from another city, because they realize that relocating to LA is a process in and of itself. There are so many stressful challenges that come with moving here: finding an apartment, learning your way around, getting used to the traffic, dealing with leaving your family and friends. It is much easier to hire a model who has already overcome these circumstances. It's okay if you aren't originally from Los Angeles. Hardly anyone is. As a matter of fact, that could be an asset.

It might make you stand out to the Producers. Living in LA has its perks, but it also brings with it a certain degree of cynicism, and perhaps, harshness to a person. A fresh, clean face, from small town USA, might be a refreshing sight for a Casting Director's sore eyes.

However, I would be afraid to tell them, for example, "I just flew in from Missouri to come to the *Deal or No Deal* audition. I'm a huge fan of the show, and I am ready to move to Los Angeles if you hire me." It might make you look enthusiastic and even demonstrate your determination; but it might also make them rule you out immediately. They may see you as naive and inexperienced, or they might fear that (even *if* they hired you), you could change your mind and decide not to move after all. They might say, "We really like you, but come back and see us once you have moved here."

So, my advice, whether you are sending in a tape or coming to a casting call, is to tell them that you live in Los Angeles. Lie if you need to. You must give the illusion of stability. It's fine to say that you have just recently *relocated* here. It's fine to say, "I'm originally from Campbell, Missouri. I grew up on a farm...," as long as you make it clear to them that you live in Los Angeles now. You can still have all the charm from back home, but it comes across in a more desirable package when you appear to live locally.

Another shared quality of the *Deal or No Deal* models is professionalism. They each appear to be experts in their respective fields. Being professional doesn't just apply to a career in Business, Law, or Medicine. It can apply to professional modeling as well. Most of the girls on the show are professional models and it really shows during the audition process. All of the girls come across in their interviews as confident, articulate, intelligent, and successful. They appear to be truly comfortable in their own skin. They seem relaxed. They seem unstressed and easy going. If you have lots of experience going to auditions and working modeling jobs then confidence will probably come naturally. If you don't have much experience, it might be a little more difficult to muster. But whether you have much professional modeling experience or not, you must appear as if you do. How do you do that?

I'm referring to exaggerating. (You can call it lying if you want to, but I prefer to think of it as being creative. Because sometimes honesty just won't get you the job). When they ask you questions about your modeling experience, you can either be completely honest and say, "No, I haven't really done much of anything." Or you might consider embelishing the work that you have done. If you shot a swimsuit calendar, then you can say that you're a "professional swimwear model." If you have been in local commercials or in newspaper modeling ads in your hometown, well, technically, that's "professional commercials and print modeling." You get the idea. You have to *sell* yourself.

I want to share a story that I was told a few years ago during a dinner party in Palm Springs, CA at the home of an older couple who used to be in the entertainment business. The woman had been a famous model and was on the cover of Vogue back in the 50's, and the man was once the leading man on the most popular Television show in the same decade. He was one of the highest paid actors of the time. He told me the story of how he first got started. He said that he had so much trouble booking jobs in either New York or Los Angeles. He was absolutely broke. So, he came up with a little lie he would tell Casting Directors that would get him hired. Every time he would audition for anything in New York, he would say, "I just flew in yesterday from Los Angeles. I was filming a movie over there." And he would do the same to the LA Casting Directors, "I just flew in from New York where I was filming a show out there." He told me that every audition he went to, he would lie and tell them that he had just flown into town. He said that he invented so many movies, TV, and Broadway shows that he was either "working on" or had "just completed" that he actually got himself confused. But it worked. It made him look "in demand," and it gave him a career. You have to have kindling to start a fire. Sometimes, it takes just one little thing to open up a lot of doors. If you can hurry the process along with a few little white lies, more power to you.

I personally never lied during my interview with *Deal or No Deal* (that I can recall), but I was also already a professional model who had appeared in numerous ad campaigns, been on the cover of Best Body Magazine, and had spreads in several other magazines. So, that was enough experience to impress them. But, to be perfectly honest (in order to get those things), I've had to get a little creative myself a time or two. Here's an example:

When I first began modeling, I was introduced to a magazine through a modeling agency. I was impressed by their photo layouts (they were MAXIM style), and I was trying to build up my modeling portfolio. So, I went in for an interview to meet the Editor. Only to realize that it was a Hispanic Men's Magazine that focused solely on *Latino women*. (Oops.)

Now, I'm from Missouri, and I don't really have a nationality other than, "American." (My Mom's side has a French last name and my Dad's side has Scottish, English, and maybe a teeny bit Spanish. There are also rumors that we have Native American somewhere, but nobody really knows for sure.) Anyway, I had been hired several times already for modeling jobs as the "Hispanic model." And, I figured I could pass as one. So I stressed to the Editor that I had some Spanish blood in my background. (Somewhere on my Dad's side). He smiled and said, "That's what all the girls tell me." I feigned a laugh and tried not to look too guilty as I asked him to explain. He said, "Everyone tells me that they have a Spanish Grandma, so they can get in our magazine." When I left his office, he told me that he really liked my look and would like to do a spread on me. But he would have to get back to me.

A couple of days later, my agent called. He said that the Editor of the magazine had really liked me, but that he couldn't do a spread on me because he didn't feel I was "Latin" enough. The news left me a little disappointed, but I was determined to get in that magazine! (I wanted those photos!)

So, a couple weeks later, I called their offices up again. The Editor wasn't in, and I ended up leaving him a message.

I told him that my agent had called me and explained that his magazine didn't feel that I was "ethnic" enough. I told him that I didn't know what he was talking about, because my father was born in Navidad, Mexico. (I know it sounds insane to make up something like that; but in my defense I had just gone on vacation in Navidad, Mexico. So, I had at least experienced a little bit of their culture?) I figured, what's the worst thing that can happen? The Editor thinks I'm crazy, and he doesn't call me back? Oh, well. As things were, I wasn't going to be in their magazine anyway. At least with my lie, I might stand a chance.

The Editor ended up calling me back, and told me that he had got my message about my "Mexican father;" but that he was a little confused. He said, he had found my paperwork and photos from our earlier meeting, but that he had written down that I wasn't Hispanic at all. (I was speechless for a moment and pretended my cellphone cut out). I felt guilty lying directly to him on the phone, so I just started sidestepping the issue. I started laughing and I said, "Yeah, you really *must* have been confused! You must have mixed me up with somebody else. That's so strange." When he asked me about Navidad, I told him, "It's a lovely place, and I was just there last month. I really try to get back once a year." When he asked me if I spoke Spanish, I started laughing and pretended my phone cut out again. Basically, when he asked me something I couldn't answer, I would interrupt him with a random question that would quickly change the subject. By the end of our conversation, I was a nervous wreck, and he was thoroughly confused; but we were scheduling my photo shoot!

By the time that the photo spread came out in the magazine, my "Mexican heritage" was long forgotten. They included my nationality as it really was. (Or as best as my family can figure it out anyway.)

So, I'm definately not advocating lying as a way of life, but if it helps you get a job here or there then it might be helpful. And it's apparently very common in this business. It doesn't make you a bad person, just a good businessman. We've all heard the old adage, "It's not who you are, but who you know." And that's true. In this case, it just happens to be, "It's not what you've done, but what they think you've done."

A final characteristic, that I feel is important to possess in order to be hired as a *Deal or No Deal* model, is a positive attitude. The Producers are looking for girls that are friendly and enthusiastic about being a part of the show. They are looking for girls who are fun, easy to work with, and down to earth. So, relax. Be yourself. Let your true, unique personality come through. I'm sure that if you let them see who you really are, they will have no choice but to hire you!

CHAPTER 22

HOW TO BECOME A DEAL OR NO DEAL CONTESTANT

There are two ways of becoming a *Deal or No Deal* contestant. One way is to submit an application to NBC's *Deal or No Deal* Casting Associates by following the guidelines found at *http://www.nbc.com/casting/#dond3*. Along with a questionnaire and a recent photo, you must send in a five minute videotape of yourself and the people whom you wish to appear with you on the show (your supporters.) In the videotape you must explain a little bit about yourself, and what you would do with a million dollars.

Another way to become a contestant is by attending one of the open auditions for *Deal or No Deal* that are held in different cities around the country. The Producers described them to us as,

"American Idol-like," in that thousands of people show up, get in line, and one by one they meet the Producers and /or Casting Associates. And they only have a very limited time to talk with each applicant. (About two minutes.)

Regardless of which audition process you choose, you must do something to stand out to the Producers, and that doesn't mean being fake, phony, or overly enthusiastic. They are looking for all types of people. It might be someone who looks very unusual, or someone who looks like the, "Average Joe." Whatever makes you unique, special, or sets you apart from the crowd make sure you share it! If you have a particular need for money then tell them. Thinking back, I remember some of the contestants who stood out to me on the show: one girl was over a hundred thousand dollars in debt from her student loans, one lady had just recovered from a lung transplant, one man was a huge NHL fan, one woman was physic, one woman wanted to open her own bakery, one man wanted to take his wife on the honeymoon they never had, one woman's husband was in the military and stationed in Iraq, one girl wanted to buy a HUMMER, one man wanted to buy a Harley Davidson.

Each and every contestant has something unique about them that makes them memorable, and *you* do too! Whatever it is that you are passionate about—let them know. If you are a housewife, but you always wanted to become a trapeze artist—let them know. Maybe you play the piano for your church, or maybe you bake the best peach pies at your county fair, or maybe you raise donkeys, or maybe you were your Homecoming Queen of your high school back in 1955, or maybe you have a pet iguana, or maybe you were a hippie and went to Woodstock, or maybe you live in a two hundred square foot apartment in New York City, maybe you love going to yard sales, or you collect old coins, or maybe you love to fish, or maybe you have ten grandchildren. Whatever it is! You have something special about you that makes you the perfect contestant for *Deal or No Deal*. You just need to figure out what it is and video tape it. The million dollars could and *should* be yours! Don't miss your opportunity. You might as well give it a shot. What do you have to lose?

(One word of caution.) You can't know anyone who works at NBC or on *Deal or No Deal* if you want to become a contestant. Say, for example, you happen to know someone, who knows someone, who happens to have met one of the models before. Don't tell them, or you might be automatically disqualified. The Producers told us instances in which this happened. They didn't feel that the contestants knew the models directly, but they couldn't take any chances. They have to make sure that the show is completely fair. That being said... go ahead, go grab a video camera, and good luck. You might just walk away with the million dollar case!

Afterward

Thank you for purchasing this copy of *Behind the Briefcase.*

Whether you're interested in becoming a model, an actor, a contestant on *Deal or No Deal,* or if you're simply a fan of the show; I sincerely hope that you have found this book both informative and enjoyable.

If you have any more questions about *Deal or No Deal* or about a career in modeling, acting, or the entertainment industry in general, please email me directly at april@aprilscott.com. It would be my pleasure to assist you in any way that I can. I look forward to hearing from you!

Good luck with all your endeavors and God Bless!

XOXO,

April Scott

FREQUENTLY ASKED QUESTIONS

Just for fun. Here are a collection of questions that I am frequently asked in magazine, radio, and TV interviews (and these are my honest answers).

What are some of your favorite movies?

When I was growing up I loved, *The Wizard of Oz*, and *Gone With the Wind,* and the Hallmark Hall of Fame version of, *The Secret Garden*. When I turned 14, my favorite movie was, *Scarface*. (And I'm still a big fan.) I also love, *Goodfellas, The DeerHunter*, and almost all of the Stanley Kubrick films: *Dr. Strangelove, A Clockwork Orange, 2001: A Space Odyssey,* and *Full Metal Jacket*. I also like a lot of older movies by Ingmar Bergman and Fellini. And I *love* all of the Monty Python and Mel Brooks movies!

What are some of your favorite TV shows?

I love to laugh, so I really enjoy watching, *Family Guy*, and *The Simpsons*. I also like re-runs of great sitcoms like: *Monty Python's Flying Circus, Three's Company, MASH,* and even *The Golden Girls*. I also watch those programs on the History channel about ancient civilizations (Egypt, Rome, Greece). And I like those shows about the paranormal with the ghost hunters on the Sci Fi and Travel channels. And I'm a little embarrassed to admit that I didn't miss one episode of VH1's reality series, *"Rock of Love—with Bret Michaels."* (He's the lead singer of the 80's hair band Poison.) It was a bunch of laughs!

What is your nationality?

I'm from southeast Missouri and I'm just a plain 'ole American. We're not really sure what our background is. We know my mom's last name is French and my dad's is Scottish. (My mom has blonde hair and blue eyes by the way.) We also know that my Grandma's last name was English. We think we might have some Native American and maybe some Spanish somewhere, but we don't have any formal records of anything. I'm Missourian.

Do you have any brother or sisters?

Yes, I have one sister who is seven years older than me. She is married and has a three year old son. She's a Biological Engineer, but she also enjoys writing screenplays.

If you could change one thing about yourself (but nothing physical), what would it be?

I would have more confidence when I meet people. Sometimes, I get quiet and shy when I get around new people or when I'm around big groups. I lose the confidence to say the things that I want to say. It doesn't always happen to me, but on occasion it does. If I could change that I would.

What do you think is your best physical feature?

I don't know that I particularly have a best feature. I personally like my eyes, because they are pretty big and expressive. (Although I have always wished that they weren't brown. I always wanted blue or green. But I guess you always want the opposite of what you have!)

You seem pretty comfortable posing in swimsuits and lingerie; would you ever consider posing for Playboy Magazine?

You know, I am pretty comfortable posing in lingerie and swimwear. But that's *totally* different than being completely nude! If Playboy called me today, I might consider it, but I can't say that I would do it. Maybe I'm too old fashioned or conservative, but I just don't personally feel right about doing that magazine.

What accomplishment are you most proud of in your life?

That's a toss up. I have to say that having the opportunity to play Daisy Duke in a film was a big treat for me. I grew up watching the Television series, and I was such a big fan of Catherine Bach (the original Daisy Duke). I was really proud to be a part of the film. But also I graduated Valedictorian of my college class of over 400 students, and I'm really proud of that too. It's not that I was super smart or even disciplined; it was a lot of staying up all night long cramming!!!

You played Daisy Duke in the most recent *Dukes of Hazzard* film. You were the third Daisy. (The first played by Catherine Bach and the second by Jessica Simpson.) What was it like to step into those Daisy Dukes, and what did you do to prepare for the role?

I was so excited when I found out that I was hired for the film. My family and I were big fans of the TV series. I grew up playing with *The Dukes of Hazzard* toy cars. I never dreamed that I would one day have an opportunity to play a role like that.

For, *The Dukes of Hazzard: The Beginning*, I was portraying Daisy at age 18, and I really wanted to stay true to the original series. I had watched Jessica Simpson, in the first movie, as the sexier, blonde, almost ditzy Daisy. It was an interesting choice, but I wanted to see the character return to the brunette, more intelligent, Daisy.

I think that one of the reasons that Catherine Bach was so memorable in that role was that her Daisy was beautiful and sexy, but in a very natural and down to earth way. I wanted to capture that side of her too.

What was it like to wear those Daisy Dukes?

I'm not going to lie, they were really short! I went to the gym six days a week the month before we started shooting.

I noticed you had a kissing scene in the new *Dukes of Hazzard* movie; do you get nervous when you have to do a scene like that?

Yes! For the Dukes movie, I was literally introduced to the guy I had to make out with *five minutes* before we were going to rehearse the scene. We were like, "Hi, nice to meet you. Okay, I'm gonna kiss you now." And with forty people in the crew standing around, it was a little embarrassing! When you are doing a love scene for a TV show or a film, it's definitely not like you're really just making out in private. It's very technical and impersonal. And *personally*, I hate them!

You have appeared on the cover of several magazines. How does it feel to see yourself on the cover of magazines such as MAXIM, Fitness RX, and Knock Out?

It's exciting! I have so much fun shooting for those magazines, and I look forward to seeing the finished product. I remember how thrilled I was to see myself in a magazine for the first time. It was on the cover of a Hairstyles magazine in 2003. I had very short hair and was wearing hotpink lipstick and a purple sweater. All in all, I looked pretty hideous, but I was still so thrilled!

Have you ever taken acting classes?

I studied Theater in college for four years and took a variety of acting classes there. I also acted in and directed several plays. When I moved to Los Angeles, I took a few acting classes on auditioning technique and had a private coach for awhile. There are so many acting classes in Los Angeles with so many actors in them. The thing is—that most of the people taking classes, aren't making a living acting. It seems like they are just wasting a lot of energy, time, and money. Acting is such a competitive field with hundreds of people auditioning for the very same parts, so it's really a crap shoot anyway. You have to have a solid acting foundation; but classes alone won't book you work.

What is it like getting photographed on the red carpet?

At first, it can be pretty intimidating because all the photographers are yelling your name. You have to look here and over there, and sometimes it's disorienting with all the flashes going off. I try not to let it stress me out and just have fun with it.

Are there any foods you stay away from?

I stay away from fast food. I don't like to eat junk food or things that are just generally unhealthy. I try to put nutritional food in my body whenever I can. If I read a food label at the grocery store that says something has more fat than it has protein in it, I usually won't buy it.

Are there any foods you can't live without?

I eat lots of pasta, ravioli, pizza, and cheese. I also love guacamole and chips. But it has to be freshly-made guacamole. (Either I have to make it myself, or they have to make it at your table in the restaurant. I don't know what it is about guacamole, but if it sits too long it's just no good.) But more than anything else, I love iced tea. (I guess it's a southern thing.) Just plain Lipton iced tea (unsweetened). I drink it constantly!

Do you ever miss your hometown?

I can't say that I really miss living in my hometown. I like to go back and visit once or twice a year. I miss my family and the people there, but not so much the small town life. I also miss the peace and quiet of living out in the country on the farm. The air is so much cleaner there than here in Los Angeles.

What do the people back home think about your success?

I have to say that the people back home are really supportive. They seem pretty proud. I have heard that they have an autographed 8x10 of me (as Daisy Duke) hanging on the wall at the local video store next to my *Dukes of Hazzard* DVD. I even made it into my hometown newspaper. (It's only eight pages long, but still I made the cover!)

Would you ever move back to your hometown?

Well, never say never, but I don't think I would ever move back to Missouri. I might go back and visit for a while, but I like living in a big city better.

What's the last book you're read?

I can hardly remember the last fiction book I read. I think it was, *The Picture of Dorian Gray.* I usually read non-fiction.
I'm a sucker for those positive thinking, self-improvement type books. I also read a great book on philosophers not too long ago. It was basically a general introduction to every major philosopher. I really enjoyed it.

Where do you live now?

I live in Beverly Hills.

How long have you lived in Los Angeles?

I have lived here for four and a half years, but it feels like fifty.

Which do you enjoy better: modeling or acting?

I enjoy them both, but for different reasons. I like modeling more some days, because it's more laid back. There are no lines to memorize or rehearse. I just show up and get to do my thing. Usually, I'm working with friends of mine, and we spend the day having fun!

(Even if, we are working really hard.) Acting is definitely more challenging, but I think that ultimately it offers more in return. It is a lot of work. But it's a more powerful medium of expression, and it is more fulfilling on a creative and intellectual level. It's *definitely* my passion.

ABOUT THE AUTHOR

April Scott is originally from Campbell, Missouri. She graduated with her B.S. in Theater from, *The College of the Ozarks,* in 2001.

She has appeared in numerous magazines, films, and Television shows, (*CSI Miami, Deal or No Deal, The Dukes of Hazzard: The Beginning*, People Magazine's 100 Most Beautiful People, Maxim Magazine's Hot 100.) She currently resides in Beverly Hills, CA.

For further information about April or her work, please visit her website ***www.aprilscott.com***; or write the following address:

ZaaGaa Productions, Inc.
C/O April Scott
P.O. Box 5775
Beverly Hills, CA 90209

ZaaGaa Productions
ZGP

To order additional copies of **Behind The Briefcase** or other April Scott titles, please call (310) 858-8410 or visit our website: www.zaagaaproductions.com. Author autographed copies are available at shop.aprilscott.com.